India in the G20

This book analyses the importance of the G20 to India, its role so far, and how it can leverage its presidency year to be an influential author of new global rules.

In 2023, India will be the President of the G20 Summit, the world's most influential multilateral economic forum. For countries like India, the G20 is a unique global institution, where developed and developing countries have equal stature. This creates opportunities to showcase their global political, economic and intellectual leadership, have a significant impact on the global economic governance agenda and make it more inclusive. This volume discusses how the Presidency year gives India the opportunity to "... hold the pen, write the rules" and lead the G20 year intellectually, financially, managerially and administratively. It provides a ringside view of India's path to the G20 Presidency and examines issues such as the core agenda of the G20; explains the significance of forums like T20, B20, and their proliferations; India's journey as a marginal player in the G20 to its current status; issue of dedicated leadership and management; and India's Agenda for 2023.

Topical, timely, important and lucidly written based on years of active initiative and participation in the G20, this book in *The Gateway House Guide to India in the 2020s* series will be key reading for scholars and researchers of economics, multilaterals, global governance, strategic studies, defence studies, SAARC, UN Studies, foreign policy, international relations, international economics and international trade, as well as interest to policymakers, diplomats, career bureaucrats, and professionals working with think tanks, academia and multilateral agencies, and business.

Manjeet Kripalani is co-founder, Gateway House: Indian Council on Global Relations. Kripalani was India Bureau chief of *Businessweek*, worked at *Worth* and *Forbes* magazines, New York, and won several awards including Gerald Loeb, George Polk, Overseas Press Club, Daniel Pearl Awards. Kripalani was 2006–2007 Edward R. Murrow Press Fellow, Council on Foreign Relations, New York. She was deputy press secretary to U.S. Presidential candidate Steve Forbes in 1995; press secretary/advisor to Meera Sanyal, independent candidate, Lok Sabha, 2008, 2014. Kripalani holds bachelor's degrees in law, English and History, Bombay University, India; Master's in International Affairs, Columbia University, New York, USA.

The Gateway House Guide to India in the 2020s

Series Editor: **Manjeet Kripalani***, co-founder, Gateway House: Indian Council on Global Relations*

The Gateway House Guide to India in the 2020s explores the connections between India's globalist past to the strengths it has developed as it steps into the future, starting with the decade of the 2020s. The volumes in this series discuss a wide range of topics, which include solutions for energy independence and environmental preservation, exposition of the new frontiers in space and technology, India's trade networks, security, foreign policies, and international relations. Furthermore, the series examines the embedded trading and entrepreneurial communities which are coming together to influence global agenda-setting and institution-building through platforms like the G20 and UN Security Council, where India will take leadership roles in this decade, in the Post-COVID-19 pandemic world.

This series appeals to an international audience, and is directed to policy-makers, think tanks, bureaucrats, professionals working in the area of politics; scholars and researchers of political science, international relations, foreign policy, world economy, politics and technology, Asian politics, South Asia studies, and contemporary history; students and the general reader, seeking an understanding of what will drive India's positioning in world affairs.

Mercantile Bombay
A Journey of Trade, Finance and Enterprise
Sifra Lentin

India and the Changing Geopolitics of Oil
Amit Bhandari

For more information about this series, please visit: https://www.routledge.com/The-Gateway-House-Guide-to-India-in-the-2020s/book-series/GHGI20

India in the G20

Rule-taker to Rule-maker

Edited by
Manjeet Kripalani

Routledge
Taylor & Francis Group

LONDON AND NEW YORK

First published 2022
by Routledge
2 Park Square, Milton Park, Abingdon, Oxon OX14 4RN

and by Routledge
605 Third Avenue, New York, NY 10158

Routledge is an imprint of the Taylor & Francis Group, an informa business
© 2022 Gateway House: Indian Council on Global Relations

British Library Cataloguing-in-Publication Data
A catalogue record for this book is available from the British Library

Library of Congress Cataloging-in-Publication Data
A catalog record has been requested for this book

ISBN: 978-0-367-60842-2 (hbk)
ISBN: 978-0-367-71611-0 (pbk)
ISBN: 978-1-003-15290-3 (ebk)

DOI: 10.4324/9781003152903

Typeset in Times New Roman
by codeMantra

Contents

Tables

Contributors

Sanjay Anandaram is Global Ambassador, iSprit, and Executive Board Member, Modular Open Source Identity Platform (MOSIP)

Amit Bhandari is the Energy and Environment Fellow, Gateway House. He worked in business media and financial markets, starting at the *Economic Times*, helped set up *ET Now*, and was research analyst at CLSA India. He has an MBA from IIM-Ahmedabad and a Bachelor's in Technology from IIT-BHU.

Rajiv Bhatia, former Ambassador, is a Distinguished Fellow, Foreign Policy Studies Programme, Gateway House: Indian Council on Global Relations, Mumbai.

Chaitanya Giri is Fellow, Space and Ocean Studies, Gateway House. A planetary and astromaterials scientist, he was affiliated with Earth-Life Science Institute, Tokyo Institute of Technology and was a Fellow at NASA Goddard Space Flight Center and Max Planck Institute, Germany.

Ambika Khanna is former Senior Researcher, International Law Studies Programme, Gateway House: Indian Council on Global Relations, Mumbai.

Akshay Mathur is former Director of Research, Gateway House. Prior to this, he was a Principal Architect with the corporate strategy group at Fidelity Investments, Boston. He has an MBA from Boston University and a BS in computer science from University of Massachusetts, Amherst, USA.

Purvaja Modak is former Researcher, Geoeconomic Studies, Gateway House. She has a Master's degree in Economics from University of Mumbai and a Bachelor's in Economics from Jai Hind College, Mumbai.

Sameer Patil is Fellow, International Security Studies, Gateway House. Prior to this, he was Assistant Director at the National Security Council Secretariat in Prime Minister's Office, New Delhi; he has completed his PhD from JNU, on India's nuclear decision-making.

Acronyms

BIS	Bank for International Settlements
ECB	European Central Bank
FAO	Food and Agriculture Organization
FATF	Financial Action Task Force
ICAO	International Civil Aviation Organization
IMF	International Monetary Fund
ITU	International Telecom Union
LIDC	Low-Income Developing Countries
OECD	Organisation for Economic Co-operation and Development
UN	United Nations
UNIDP	UN Industrial Development Organization
WIPO	World Intellectual Property Organization
WTO	World Trade Organization

1 What is the G20, and why it is important

1.1 The core agenda of the G20

The Group of Twenty, or G20, was conceptualised during the Asian financial crisis of 1997. It comprises 19 countries plus one bloc, the European Union. The finance ministers and central bank governors of member countries met in Germany in 1999 for a broad-based discussion on containing the effects of the crisis through collective measures by developed and developing countries.

When the trans-Atlantic crisis hit Western economies in 2008, the forum was upgraded to a head of state summit. Pushed by the affected Western economies, the G20 took collective decisions to stabilise the world economy and came to be acknowledged as the worlds "premier economic governance platform."[1] India and China gained prominence during this time for their generous contributions in helping to bail out affected countries.

Today, the G20 is the world's most powerful economic body. Its members combine over 80% of world GDP, 75% of global trade and 60% of the population. Its core agenda is the world economy and global economic leadership. Post 2008, it is also focused on creating rules and institutions that will prevent another financial crisis. Now, with the existing multilateral order like the United Nations (UN) and the World Trade Organization (WTO) weakening and its authority contested, other pressing global issues are also discussed at the G20.

As the Organisation of Economic Co-operation and Development (OECD) describes it, "the G20 has organically evolved, transforming itself from a global firefighter into a unique international forum to address long-term structural challenges."[2]

Emerging economies like India describe the G20's role in clearly financial and futuristic terms. The Ministry of External Affairs, India, says the objective of the G20 is "to create a new international financial

DOI: 10.4324/9781003152903-1

structure," coordinate policy between members to "achieve global economic stability, sustainable growth" and "promote financial regulations that reduce risks and prevent future financial crises."[3]

The G20 has no secretariat and functions through a revolving presidency chosen through rotating regional groups. The closest to a secretariat of the G20 is the OECD, which refers to itself as "an active partner and strategic advisor" to the G20.[4] It contributes significantly, by

> helping to define the agenda and developing narratives, providing policy options and preparing evidence-based analysis and reports, forging consensus across the membership around Presidency's priorities, strengthening the global governance by setting global standard on key issues, ensuring that legacies and commitments from previous Presidencies are monitored and delivered.[5]

Related entities, like the Inter-Agency Group on Economic and Financial Statistics Non-government bodies, also study, prepare, analyse and record the G20's confabulations. Outside of the OECD, the other institution that significantly does this is the G20 Information Centre at the University of Toronto.[6]

Each country assigns a "Sherpa" to represent itself in the G20 collaborations that lead up to the leaders' summit. The OECD has its own permanent G20 "Sherpa" or representative to the G20.

Currently, the leadership of the G20 is managed under a "troika" system made up of the immediate past, current president and next host countries. In 2021, the troika will be Saudi Arabia (immediate past president), Italy (current president) and Indonesia (next host).

Countries define the priorities of their presidency early, usually a year in advance. In defining their agendas, countries work closely with their chambers of commerce, enterprise forums, businesses, academic institutions and policymakers. Research papers are circulated a year in advance. The G20 chairs create catchy phrases and often highlight some of their domestic agendas.

For instance, Turkey defined the priorities of its presidency on the principles of Inclusiveness, Implementation and Investment. It included the development of Micro, Small and Medium Enterprises (MSME) through Low-Income Developing Countries (LIDC) participation in global supply chains.[7] This is Turkey's strength. Turkish MSMEs contribute over 50% to the country's GDP and provide over 70% of employment, making the sector a significant player in the country's economic agenda.[8]

Germany's preoccupation with the issue of economic and political migrants – it accepted an estimated 1 million refugees[9] from across Syria, Iraq and Africa in 2015 – resulted in a focus on migration and refugee flows from Africa.[10] It became the G20's Compact with Africa[11]

In 2021, Italy's agenda is People, Planet and Prosperity.[12] It will carry forward a new agenda item for the G20, i.e. culture or the Cultural Economy, which was discussed on the side lines of the November 4 meeting[13] hosted by past president of Saudi Arabia. It reflects the Saudi Kingdom's on-going opening up of its society and country to the world, as also Italy's dominant economic sector, tourism, on which it will depend for growth and employment, as the pandemic recedes.

The G20 Presidency year closes with the annual leaders' summit – a prestigious event where the leaders of the G20 countries and their entourage including ministers, central bankers and diplomats – descend on the host country for a giant, high-profile family meeting of consensus seekers.

Table 1.1 List of G20 presidents and summit venues since 2008

Year	Date	G20 Presidency	Summit Venue
2008	14–15 November	Brazil	Washington, DC, USA
2009	1–2 April	United Kingdom	London, UK
	24–25 September	United Kingdom	Pittsburgh, Pennsylvania, USA
2010	26–27 June	Republic of Korea	Toronto, Canada
	11–12 November	Republic of Korea	Seoul, Korea
2011	3–4 November	France	Cannes, France
2012	18–19 June	Mexico	Los Cabos, Mexico
2013	5–6 September	Russia	St Petersburg, Russia
2014	15–16 November	Australia	Brisbane, Australia
2015	15–16 November	Turkey	Antalya, Turkey
2016	4–5 September	China	Hangzhou, China
2017	7–8 July	Germany	Hamburg, Germany
2018	30 November–1 December	Argentina	Buenos Aires, Argentina
2019	28–29 June	Japan	Osaka, Japan
2020	21–22 November	Saudi Arabia	Virtual Summit
2021	30–31 October	Italy	Rome, Italy
2022	October	Republic of Indonesia	

Source: Collated by Gateway House from various sources.

1.2 Who leads the G20

Within countries, three ministries are central to G20 participation. The head of government – the Prime Minister's/President's office – actively leads the global economic governance agenda, along with the three main offices of the executive branch of government: the central bank (Reserve Bank of India), the finance ministry and the external affairs ministry. They are assisted by a dozen line ministries like commerce, agriculture, energy and labour.

It requires energy, strategic planning, high-level ministerial, sub-ministerial and sub-forum meetings, task forces, participating in negotiation and feedback.

1.3 The many parts of the G20 and their proliferations

The G20 comprises working tracks, engagement groups and working groups. These have proliferated over the years, with several overlaps.

Table 1.2 India's G20 Heads of State, Finance Ministers and Sherpas since 2010

Year	Heads of State	Finance Ministers	Sherpas
2010	Dr. Manmohan Singh	Pranab Mukherjee	Montek Singh Ahluwalia
2011	Dr. Manmohan Singh	Pranab Mukherjee	
2012	Dr. Manmohan Singh	Pranab Mukherjee	
	Dr. Manmohan Singh	Manmohan Singh	
	Dr. Manmohan Singh	P. Chidambaram	
2013	Dr. Manmohan Singh	P. Chidambaram	
2014	Dr. Manmohan Singh	P. Chidambaram	Suresh Prabhu
	Narendra Modi	Arun Jaitley	
2015	Narendra Modi	Arun Jaitley	Arvind Panagariya
2016	Narendra Modi	Arun Jaitley	
2017	Narendra Modi	Arun Jaitley	
2018	Narendra Modi	Arun Jaitley	
2019	Narendra Modi	Arun Jaitley	Suresh Prabhu

Source: Collated by Gateway House from various sources.

1.3.1 Working tracks

There are two working tracks: the finance track and the Sherpa track.

The **finance track** continues the work of the pre-2008 G20 agenda led by the finance ministers and central bank governors. Its job is to focus on purely financial issues like financial regulation, international taxation, monetary and fiscal policies, exchange rates and infrastructure investment.

The finance track is led by the respective finance ministers and central bank governors as well as representatives of various ministries of finance.

The **Sherpa track** focuses on the expanded G20 agenda, which is more political and focused on development, digitisation, issues of corruption, energy, climate risk and now health and the post-COVID-19 response.

The Sherpa, considered the personal emissary of the country's leader, is typically a senior government official, or diplomat, and sometimes a political appointee with government experience. The Sherpa is assisted by a "sous sherpa" usually a serving, senior diplomat.

Together, the two tracks prepare the leaders' communique at the end of the G20 year.

1.3.2 Engagement groups

The Engagement groups represent other parts of society and the economy, whose recommendations can help the central G20 agenda. They work independently from governments. Over the years, the engagement groups have grown in number, as each country seeks to put its stamp on its presidency year. The core engagement groups are the Business 20 (B20), Civil 20 (C20), Youth 20 (Y20), Labour 20 (L20), Think (Tank) 20 (T20), Women 20 (W20), Science 20 (S20) and Urban 20 (U20). Each one of these conducts its own Task Forces, consultations and partnerships.[14]

Countries often assign Sherpa status to organisations and institutions which lead these engagements. For instance, the leading chamber of commerce of a country is typically the Business 20 Sherpa – in India, it will be the CII, or Chamber of Commerce and Industry. The T20, or Think Tank 20, is a network of think tanks and researchers that supports the government in agenda-building and shaping and produces policy briefs that often find their way into the Leaders' final communiqué[15] (Mathur 2016). The T20 Sherpa institution will typically have expertise in cross-disciplinary issues. For instance, Germany had two

T20 sherpas, the privately run Kiel Institute for the Global Economy and the state-supported DIE (The German Development Institute).

1.3.3 Working groups

The Working Groups comprise experts from individual the G20 countries, tasked with addressing specific issues across a wide swathe of sectors, from agriculture to environment, infrastructure, anti-corruption and now recently, to include culture and labour. These groups are often outside of the official system, but with deep expertise, and conduct their own meetings. They develop Issue Briefs which also, ultimately, feed into the Leaders' communique at the end of the G20 year.[16]

On average, each presidency has had approximately six working groups. The chairmanship, agenda, proceedings and outcomes of each of the groups have to be managed by the G20 host country. The host country can also assign a working group to another G20 country. For instance, under the French Presidency in 2011, President Nicolas Sarkozy requested Germany to chair the group on the international monetary system in 2011 along with Mexico.[ii]

An important working group is the Framework Working Group (FWG), which was created at the Pittsburgh Summit in 2009. Its focus is to promote and coordinate national growth strategies and economic policies. It's officially called the Pittsburgh Process for "strong, sustainable and balanced growth."

It is under this working group that India has been able to contribute to – and achieve its own goals on – issues like black money (Beneficial Ownership rules) and Non-Cooperative Jurisdiction (Financial Action Task Force or FATF), new benchmarks and a new global financial architecture (Financial Stability Board or FSB, International Accounting Standards Board or IASB).

India has hosted four FWG meetings on its own soil: in Neemrana, Delhi, in 2012 (under the Mexican Presidency), Goa in 2014 (Australian Presidency), Kerala in 2015 (Turkish Presidency) and Varanasi in 2017 (German Presidency). In 2020, India's Chief Economic Advisor, Sanjeev Sanyal, co-chaired the Framework Working Group along with his U.K. counterpart. The express purpose was economic recovery post the COVID-19 pandemic.

1.4 The participating institutions of the G20

Like the UN, the G20 has several participating institutions. The most well-known are the OECD, the Financial Stability Board (FSB), World Bank (WB), the International Monetary Fund (IMF), the WTO and

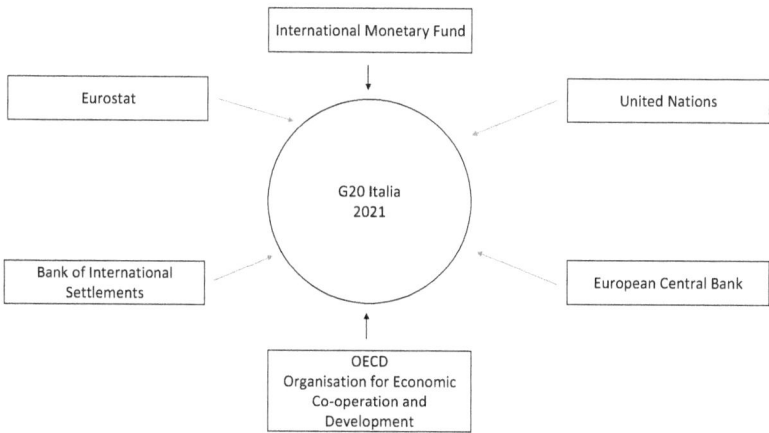

Figure 1.1 The participating institutions of the G20.
Source: *Gateway House Research; Adapted from a graphic by Dakshta Ahlawat.*

the International Labour Organization (ILO). Their representatives attend the G20 meetings regularly as well as provide expert support, take on assignments and prepare reports and position papers on the G20 agendas, past, present and future.

These make significant, on-going contributions. For instance, the Inter-Agency Group (IAG) on Economic and Financial Statistics was formed in 2008 to monitor economic and financial developments in "significant countries."[17] The AGI is made up of representatives from the important participating international organisations, viz. Bank for International Settlements (BIS), the European Central Bank (ECB), Eurostat, the IMF, the OECD, the UN and the World Bank. Its early agenda was to identify and plug information data gaps, and a Data Gap Initiative was formed for this.[18]

Outside of these institutions, non-government bodies like think tanks and academia are significantly involved. They study, prepare, analyse and record the G20's confabulations. One with a significant body of G20 work is the G20 Information Centre at the University of Toronto.[19]

Notes

1 "G20 Leaders Statement: The Pittsburgh Summit", G20 Information Centre, University of Toronto, http://www.g20.utoronto.ca/2009/2009communique0925.html

2 OCED. *OCED-G20*. n.d. https://www.oecd.org/g20/about/ (accessed 01 18, 2021).
3 Ministry of External Affairs, Government of India. "G20 – Group of Twenty." *Ministry of External Affairs, Government of India*. August 2012. http://www.mea.gov.in/Portal/ForeignRelation/g20-august-2012.pdf (accessed 01 18, 2021).
4 OCED. *OCED-G20*. n.d. https://www.oecd.org/g20/about/ (accessed 01 18, 2021).
5 OCED. *OCED-G20*. n.d. https://www.oecd.org/g20/about/ (accessed 01 18, 2021).
6 University of Toronto. "G20 Information Centre – About Us." *University of Toronto, G20 Centre*. n.d. http://www.g20.utoronto.ca/about.html (accessed 01 18, 2021).
7 G20 Turkey, "G20/OECD High-Level Principles on SME Financing." *G20 Antalya, Turkey*. https://ms.hmb.gov.tr/uploads/2018/11/Key-Messages.pdf (accessed 01 18, 2021).
8 European Commission. "2019 SBA Fact Sheet." *European Comission*. 2019. https://ec.europa.eu/neighbourhood-enlargement/sites/near/files/sba-fs-2019_turkey.pdf (accessed 01 18, 2021).
9 Trines, Stefan. "The State of Refugee Integration in Germany." *World Education News and Reviews*. 08 08, 2019. https://wenr.wes.org/2019/08/the-state-of-refugee-integration-in-germany-in-2019 (accessed 01 18, 2021).
10 G20 Germany. "German Presidency at a Glance." *G20 Germany*. 2017. https://www.g20germany.de/Webs/G20/EN/G20/Agenda/agenda_node.html#:~:text=Germany%20also%20wants%20to%20use,example%2C%20issues%20of%20global%20significance (accessed 01 19, 2021).
11 G20. "G20 Compact with Africa." *G20 Compact with Africa*. n.d. https://www.compactwithafrica.org/content/compactwithafrica/home.html (accessed 01 19, 2021).
12 G20. *G20 Italy Priorities*. 01 01, 2021. https://www.g20.org/ (accessed 01 18, 2021).
13 "In historic move, G20 puts culture on its agenda for the first time." *UNESCO*. 06 11, 2020. https://en.unesco.org/news/historic-move-g20-puts-culture-its-agenda-first-time (accessed 01 18, 2021).
14 Urban20 Riyadh. *Circular Carbon Neutral Economy*. 2020. https://www.urban20riyadh.org/taskforces/circular-carbon-neutral-economy (accessed 01 18, 2021).
15 Mathur, Akshay. "T20 – Thinking for G20." *Gateway House – Indian Council on Global Relations*. 08 04, 2016. https://www.gatewayhouse.in/t20-thinking-g20/ (accessed 01 18, 2021).
16 Climate Action Network International. "G20 Working Group – Issue Briefs." *Climate Action Network International*. n.d. http://www.climate-network.org/working-group-pages/g20 (accessed 01 18, 2021).
17 IMF. "Press Release: Inter-Agency Group on Economic and Financial Statistics Launches Enhanced G-20 Statistical Web Site, IMF Announces." *International Monetary Fund*. 12 22, 2009. https://www.imf.org/en/News/Articles/2015/09/14/01/49/pr09474#:~:text=The%20Inter%2D-Agency%20Group%20on%20Economic%20and%20Financial%20Statistics%20was,Nations%2C%20and%20the%20World%20Bank (accessed 01 18, 2021).

18 IMF-FSB. "Countdown to 2021 in Light of COVID-19." *International Monetary Fund*. 10 2020. https://www.imf.org/external/np/g20/pdf/2020/100720.pdf (accessed 01 18, 2021).
19 University of Toronto. "G20 Information Centre – About Us." *University of Toronto, G20 Centre*. n.d. http://www.g20.utoronto.ca/about.html (accessed 01 18, 2021).

Additional reading

"India, G20 and the World," *Ministry of Statistics and Programme Implementation, Government of India*, accessed 18 January 2021, http://mospi.nic.in/sites/default/files/Statistical_year_book_india_chapters/INDIA%2C%20G20%20AND%20THE%20WORLD%20-WRITEUP.PDF

2 2020

The G20's virtual year

Rajiv Bhatia

2.1 Introduction

In the end, the G20 in 2020 went by virtually and actively. The pandemic and health was a major focus, but the G20 didn't lose sight of its main agenda: global economic governance. Under the circumstances, Saudi Arabia steered the G20 with grit, hosting a long list of high-level virtual meetings since the virtual summit of G20 leaders in March. There were clear outcomes such as a detailed, multi-sectoral plan to fight against the COVID-19 as well as to stabilise the global economy.

In this chapter, Rajiv Bhatia follows the G20's first virtual year, including the Space 20 analysis by Chaitanya Giri, and concludes that without the endeavours of the G20, the COVID-hit world may have been worse off. And that India must step up its engagement in the forum, which it will chair in 2023.

2.1.1 The action imperative for the G20

The extraordinary summit of G20 leaders, held on 26 March 2020 by video conference, was an innovative, even historic, step. In reaffirming its commitment to present "a united front" against the virus that "respects no borders" and "to do whatever it takes to overcome the pandemic," G20 strove to send out a clear message to an anxious world. Nevertheless, as the summit ended, the question was: will lofty words result in quick and effective action?

In April, the Johns Hopkins University of Medicine world tracker on COVID-19 showed the following numbers: total confirmed cases –935,817; total deaths – 47,208. These alarming figures would increase further in the days to come.[1]

This devastating disease struck the world when the G20 nations' instinct for multilateralism and global cooperation had weakened;

DOI: 10.4324/9781003152903-2

U.S.-China recriminations were running high on a range of issues, including the name and origin of the disease and ascribing responsibility for its spread, and the World Health Organization (WHO) was under fire for its inordinately slow response and unjustifiably delayed declaration of the Coronavirus Disease (COVID-19) as a pandemic. The controversy over the name, with the U.S. keen to term it the "Chinese virus," led to the G7's failure to issue a joint statement. It, therefore, came as some consolation when the main actors finally behaved better, agreed to call it "COVID-19" and concentrated on crafting the way to fight it.

The virtual summit was prepared carefully. Separate meetings of G20 finance ministers and central bank governors and the Sherpas took place in the preceding days. The leaders' summit took place because Prime Minister Narendra Modi pushed for it, talking beforehand with the Russian president, the Australian prime minister and the president of the EU Commission, while nudging Saudi Arabia to lead the way. King Salman bin Abdulaziz Al Saud, Prime Minister of Saudi Arabia, chaired the summit graciously and effectively.

As the summit's outcome was shaped by participants' positions, a quick look at a few of them would be instructive.

First, President Xi Jinping presented his four-point formula: resoluteness to wage an all-out war, a collective response for control and treatment, active role by relevant international organisations and enhancing international micro-economic policy coordination.[2] Those looking for signs of admission of responsibility and expression of regret were in for a disappointment.

Second, PM Modi stressed "the need to put human beings at the centre of our vision of global prosperity and coordination," while championing the cause of "a new globalisation" as well as the reform of WHO.[3] New Delhi was clear that the world, facing an unprecedented crisis, had no choice but to be united and positive. It should avoid polemics, fixing its sights on a blueprint for decisive action.

Third, Dr. Tedros Adhanom Ghebreyesus, the beleaguered director general of WHO, relied on brevity to convey his message. He urged the world leaders to fight "like your lives depend on it – because they do.", to unite because no country "can solve this crisis alone" and to ignite "global production for the tools we need to save lives now."[4] He said nothing in defence of his organisation facing rising worldwide criticism over initially denying human-to-human transmission in face of evidence to the contrary and failing to advise imposition of restrictions on trade- and tourism-related traffic with China – until it was too late.

The summit's statement dealt with four key themes:

a   G20 governments agreed to commit "taking all necessary health measures" for containing the pandemic and protecting people. These range from research and development (R&D) to increasing medical supplies and strengthening WHO. Health ministers have been asked to meet and develop "a set of G20 urgent actions" for this purpose.
b   Anxious about prospects for the global economy, participants resolved to deploy "all available policy tools" to minimise the economic and social dimensions and restore global growth.
c   Worried about disruptions to the global supply chains, they agreed to cooperate in ensuring the flow of vital medical supplies as well as agricultural and other products.
d   Enhancing global cooperation was identified as another goal. A short formulation was added to highlight the special needs of "developing and least developed countries, and notably in Africa and small island states."

The statement consisted essentially of goals and aspirations at a time when the world expected and needed a solid plan of action. At least on the health-related cooperation front, there was a clarity of purpose and mention of the "COVID-19 Solidarity Response Fund," but it was voluntary in nature and contributions have been solicited from governments, international organisations and the private sector. Measures to protect the global economy were far too general and vague. The announcement of a $5-trillion injection into the world economy masks the fact that it would be nothing but a sum total of disparate national financial packages, to be devised and executed by G20 governments as they deemed fit. The reference to developing countries and Africa, lacking substance and specifics, was a mere exhortation.

These perceptions compel long-time observers of G20 to maintain that the spirit and strategy that helped vanquish the 2008–2009 financial crisis are not in evidence today; not yet, at least. The G20 statement failed "to convey a spirit of robust internationalism and multilateral cooperation," asserted a group of three eminent scholars at the Centre for Strategic International Studies (CSIS).[5]

The virtual summit was been followed by a meeting of trade ministers on 30 March, and another meeting of finance ministers. The health ministers, preoccupied with battling the pandemic at home, were to meet later in April. But by that time, the situation turned grim. Hence, the need to dramatically step up international cooperation, keeping in view the fact that the post-war world has not faced a challenge and tragedy as grave as this one.

With nearly 90% of COVID-19 confirmed cases and deaths occurring in G20 countries, its leaders stand accountable in the court of history.

2.1.2 G20 actions in the early COVID days

On 26 March 2020, at its first-ever virtual summit, the G20 resolved "to do whatever it takes to overcome the pandemic" – the Coronavirus dashboard showed a global total of 935,817 confirmed cases and 47,208 deaths. Seven weeks later, as of 20 May 2020, the figures increased dramatically to 4.89 million cases and 323,221 deaths worldwide.[6]

Did the G20 fail to deliver?

Undoubtedly, the G20 response to COVID began on a slow note. Policy analysts gave the joint statement issued after the initial summit "barely passing grade."[7] Escalating U.S.-China tensions and a striking lack of U.S. and European leadership were the key factors responsible for this. But at least the summit did take place, and it was thanks to middle players such as India, Russia and Australia that asserted themselves and coaxed G20 chair, Saudi Arabia, to convene the virtual summit.

Following that initiative all G20 member states including United States and China, laboured and persevered in crafting a substantive "G20 Action Plan" to tackle this world catastrophe. Importantly, "a-whole-of-the-government" strategy involving several national ministries was agreed upon and adopted. This helped secure agreement on early and desired actions in several crucial areas.

Ministerial collaboration: In the two months following the summit, there were 11 virtual meetings of ministers of member states across integral departments to plan and endorse collaborative efforts in their respective areas.

a   Two meetings of trade and investment ministers led to the outlining of "G20 Actions to Support World Trade and Investment Response to COVID-19," which detail both short- and long-term collective actions.[8] The former ensured that emergency trade measures did not create disruptions to global supply chains, whereas the latter promoted necessary reforms to the WTO.

b   Energy ministers agreed that the sector would continue to make a "fully effective contribution to overcoming COVID-19 and powering subsequent global recovery." They aimed to develop "collaborative policy responses" to ensure market stability across energy resources as well as to maintain the balance of interests between producers and consumers that will safeguard an uninterrupted flow of energy.[9]

c   Health ministers crafted an agreement on the steps necessary to address systemic weaknesses in health systems, improve pandemic preparedness, utilise digital solutions and improve patient safety.

d   An interesting development was the meeting of digital economy ministers, which stressed "the promising role of digital technologies and relevant digital policies" in strengthening their individual country's responses to the pandemic. Their plan covered aspects such as augmenting communication infrastructure and network connectivity, and R&D of digital technologies for health.[10]

e   Agriculture, labour and employment, and tourism ministers also had discussions to develop a cooperative framework for their respective areas.

An economic support system: Finance ministers and central bank governors occupy a special position in G20's architecture. Their collaboration is integral to the forum's effectiveness as an influential multilateral body. Two important meetings on economic concerns were held before and after the 26 March leadership summit. These meetings were instrumental in drawing up the "G20 Action Plan – Supporting the Global Economy Through the COVID-19 Pandemic."[11] The comprehensive plan covered crucial facets of health infrastructure; economy and finance; stimulating sustainable, balanced and inclusive growth and providing international support for countries in need.

One important measure finalised as part of this plan was support for the World Bank and IMF to use their instruments "as part of a coordinated global response," including "a time-bound suspension" of debt service payments for the poorest countries.[12] As a result of this decision, the debts of nations to the World Bank and the IMF, as well as debts between individual countries, would be assessed on a case-by-case basis. Payment arrangements were to be negotiated through bilateral discussions between member countries.

It is easy to be sceptical about the efficacy of the spectrum of G20's efforts in mitigating COVID-19. But no one should forget the role that G20 played in successfully resolving the global financial crisis of 2008–2009 when the United States, Europe, China, India and others worked in tandem.

Many of these important relationships fractured as a result of the pandemic, making it even more imperative for the forum to deliver results through implementation.

The inescapable fact is that G20 is the only multilateral body collaborating and attempting to tackle the crises currently. Especially, since institutions such as the UN Security Council have been completely ineffective in their approach; first, by delaying any discussion on the matter and then by convening an unproductive meeting that did not yield any results.

The G20 is the leading forum for deliberation and coordination of policy on global issues. With the world's 19 largest economies and the European Union as its members, it represents over 66% of the world population, 75% of global trade and 80% of world GDP.[13] At a time of global crisis when relations between China and the world, especially the United States, are strained, it is important that India and like-minded G20 member nations step up and build the momentum for economic collaboration towards crisis mitigation.

Despite speculations from scholars to the contrary, the understanding among insiders and practitioners of the twenty-first-century diplomacy is that every G20 member, including the United States and China, is equally invested in the forum's success and wants to contribute collectively and constructively towards positive results.

In 2023, India will chair the G20. It has the unique responsibility to prepare for the challenges this will entail as the world economy may still be reeling from the after-effects of the current crisis. India must keep an optimistic mindset and a keen eye on the changing power dynamics of the post-COVID political landscape.

2.1.3 The expectation from the B20

The G20 continues to display strength and resilience because of its intimate connections with key segments of member states viz. business, think-tanks, labour, women and others. The thinking and work of these "engagement groups"[14] help G20 leaders to make decisions that are inclusive and acceptable to large segments of their polities.

The Business20, or B20, was the first engagement group to emerge, in 2010 when the presidency was held first by Canada and then by South Korea.

As the collective business voice to G20 governments, the B20 systematically develops and transmits practical policy recommendations to governments. It is composed of business representatives from G20 countries, the special invitee countries of the host presidency and a handful of international business organisations. A total of 31 institutions participated at the B20 Tokyo summit in March 2019, under Japan's G20 Presidency.[15] India was represented by the Confederation of Indian Industry (CII).

As the G20 summit transitioned from Osaka to Riyadh, under the current Saudi G20 Presidency, a close look at the recent evolution in views and recommendations of the B20 shows how quickly the world changed.

Just a year ago, in Tokyo, business leaders were busy articulating the need for and importance of international cooperation, and the role the G20 could play to strengthen it. The B20, especially, presented a future vision anchored in realising the "Creative Society" envisaged in "Society 5.0 for Sustainable Development Goals (SDGs)."[16] The policy recommendations that emerged from this vision covered: digital transformation, trade and investment, energy and environment, quality infrastructure, health and integrity "for all"[17]

Six months later, the COVID-19 pandemic struck. One year after the G20 summer summit in Osaka, the global total of confirmed infection cases and deaths had climbed to 14.89 million and 615,465, respectively.[18] The global economy was seriously damaged and heading for contraction, with developing countries and Least Developed Countries (LDCs) being worst hit.

The catastrophe forced a fundamental shift in the deliberations and decision-making of the G20 and its engagement groups. The B20, with a sharp awareness of the pandemic's damaging implications for global health as well as the world economy, took some key actions:

a   In March 2020, an open letter representing the views of the B20, the International Chamber of Commerce (ICC) and the WHO was presented to the G20. On health, it called on G20 leaders to substantially improve experience sharing and monitoring and use the private sector to support testing. On the economy, a call was given for implementing short-and-medium fiscal policy measures to support economic activity. Governments were also advised to urgently scale up social protection for displaced and affected workers.[19]

b   B20's Saudi Arabian lead welcomed the outcome of the Extraordinary G20 Leaders' virtual summit of 26 March 2020. It also praised the G20's recognition of the useful role the private sector could play in the rapid development, monitoring and distribution of diagnostics, anti-viral medicines and vaccines to fight the pandemic.[20]

c   Through a joint statement, the B20, the Labour20 (L20) and the Women20 (W20) underlined the need for the G20 to adopt a "coordinated and gender-sensitive response to an unprecedented global health, social and economic crisis."[21]

As chair of the B20, Saudi Arabia, itself deeply impacted by COVID-19 with over 200,000 infected and over 2,500 deaths by May 2020, and historically low oil prices, confronted the twin challenge of guiding the G20 to

a pursue a comprehensive strategy on all COVID-19-related issues and
b re-focus on B20's regular agenda of economic growth.

Saudi Arabia began coordinating preparatory work under three linked themes: Women in Business, Small to Medium Enterprises (SMEs) – which account for over 90% of all businesses – and Entrepreneurship and Sustainable Development Goals (SDGs). It insisted that the empowerment of women be a top agenda item.

The Saudi chair also set up taskforces to deliberate on and craft policy recommendations for six specific themes: digitalisation; energy; sustainability and climate; finance and infrastructure; future of work and education; integrity and compliance; and trade and investment.

The entire B20 agenda in respect to the war against COVID-19, the three themes and the domains covered by the six taskforces, should have been of considerable interest to India Inc. Not only because of the expectations placed on the Riyadh summit but also by India's approaching responsibilities to take over as chair of the G20 in 2023. While CII has been driving preparations for the future on behalf of the Indian business community, it seems that there is much scope for other apex industry chambers and think-tanks to step up their engagement and contribute more pro-actively to the deliberations and ongoing work of B20. It's an opportunity of global leadership for Indian business to seize, for starting 2022, India will join the G20 Troika, the three-member country committee chaired by current summit presidency, and will be expected to pull its weight.

Neither the government nor India Inc. has time to lose. They must now work on a vision integrating India's own priorities such as "reformed multilateralism," free and fair trade based on "self-reliant" economic growth, better digital regulation and effective curbs on terrorism and international crime to shape the G20/B20 agenda of the future. They should also accelerate strategising on how to make the B20, under Indian leadership, more effective and more relevant to global needs.[22]

2.1.4 India's springboard for 2023: Africa and space

i   Bringing Africa into the G20 orbit

Africa has been finding a foothold on the G20 agenda over the past decade. This should be firmed up further in the decade of the 2020s. African issues began to seep into the G20's consciousness after 2010 when under the Korean Presidency, the Seoul Development Consensus on Shared Growth was crafted, with its emphasis on "economic growth based on private-sector development and equal partnership between low-income countries and donors."[23] The spread of the Ebola pandemic in 2014 elicited financial contributions from a few G20 countries to counter it effectively in Africa.

The 2016 summit at Hangzhou under the Chinese Presidency resulted in an articulation of strong support for the industrialisation in Africa – but no concrete action followed. It was Germany which, under its presidency in 2017, took cooperation with Africa to a new level, with a structured approach to drive the agenda anchored on the Compact with Africa (CwA).

The immediate propellant for this was the refugee crisis in Europe, the result of the wars in Syria and Libya, which also flowed in vast numbers of African refugees. China's dominating presence in Africa was the other consideration.

At the G20 summit in Hamburg 2017, this initiative was launched to persuade African countries to improve their macro-economic, business and financial environment for greater induction of foreign investments, especially in infrastructure. Only 12 African countries joined this project[24] (Floyd 2020). Three years later, the initiative has been judged to be a mixed success and "a long game."[25]

Saudi Arabia commenced its 2020 innings determined to address suitably "an ever-changing global landscape that is being transformed by technological, economic, demographic and environmental changes." Convinced that "an increasingly interconnected world" needed international collaboration more than ever before, the Saudi King observed, "The Kingdom strongly believes in the power of global cooperation to forge beneficial solutions, face challenges and create opportunities for all of humanity."[26] This well-crafted message released on 1 December 2019 carried no direct reference either to Africa or (understandably) to the COVID-19 pandemic that was to become the overarching theme during the year 2020.[27]

The November summit in Riyadh deliberated on the next phase of the war against COVID – with some reference to Africa-related subjects. For example, G20 finance ministers and central bank governors closely monitored progress of the Debt Service Suspension Initiative (DSSI) for burdened developing countries and promised to consider "possible extension" an initiative designed to benefit a sizeable number of African states.[28]

Most specifically, the Riyadh Declaration said (C.22),

> We are determined to support African countries in overcoming the crisis, including by exploring more sustainable financing options for growth in Africa. We reiterate our continued support for the G20 Initiative on Supporting the Industrialisation in Africa and the LDCs, G20 Africa Partnership and the Compact with Africa, and other relevant initiatives.[29]

What Africa needs is fairly well known. Its vision of the future was delineated in the African Union's Agenda 2063 and the UN's 2030 Agenda for Sustainable Development. In the COVID era, although Africa has been less impacted, largely due to the Ebola protocols put in place in many countries like Liberia, Ivory Coast and Nigeria, the continent requires more assistance to deal with the pandemic's adverse impact on the health sector and the economy. African countries clamour for effective relief from the escalating debt and interest burden, both multilateral and bilateral.[30]

Beyond this, there is a persistent need for global cooperation with Africa in a host of sectors: infrastructure, education and capacity building, agriculture and food security, strengthening the mechanisms of regional and continental trade, local manufacturing and employment creation, safeguards against climate change, digitisation and economic rejuvenation in genera – all areas that fall within the purview of G20. Clearly, Africa needs greater attention from the world's premier multilateral forum at this critical juncture.

Within G20, Africa's representation has been rather ineffective. Only one African country – South Africa – is its member. The AU and the New Partnership for Africa's Development (NEPAD) enjoy observer status, disappointingly more symbolic than substantive. Hence, G20's Africa linkage must be strengthened. The AU deserves to be admitted as a full member of the G20, much as the EU is. A good case can be built for the entry of at least two more African states into the G20, but this could open the Pandora's Box; hence, the AU will decidedly be a more suitable entrant.

Immediate steps can be taken by India under the 2021 G20 chair Italy, to establish an institutional mechanism for consultations with the AU. The AU Presidency can be urged to set up a group of senior officials representing select African countries (i.e. Africa's own G10 or even G20). The G20 can then launch a series of discussions with this representative group on a regular basis to ensure that Africa's feedback is brought into the G20's mainstream policymaking.[31]

This is the time for India to step up its game in Africa as a dynamic actor and lead from within the G20 to pursue a multilateral agenda that contributes to peace and prosperity on the African continent.

ii   India can democratise space for the developing world

The Kingdom of Saudi Arabia (KSA) had early on identified space co-operation as one of the key agendas of its presidency of the Group of 20 (G20) multilateral in 2020. The KSA acknowledges space technology as important for common global goods like climate and oceans, as well as an enabler of food security, global health and sustainable development.

To that end, the Saudi Space Commission, KSA's leading space policymaking body, organised the Space Economy Leaders Meeting (Space20) on October 7, with the participation of the 19 other national space agencies of the G20 member states as well as the European Space Agency and the United Nations Office for Outer Space Affairs (UNOOSA). The Saudi Presidency has asked the UNOOSA to oversee the Space20 Working Group for future presidencies.

Space20 is certainly not the first forum where space agencies of G20 nations have gathered. The UNOOSA, United Nations Committee on the Peaceful Use of Outer Space (UNCOPUOS), Space Frequency Co-ordination Group (SFCG), Inter-Agency Debris Coordination Committee (IADC), Coordination Group on Meteorological Satellites (CGMS), International Astronautical Federation (IAF), Committee on Space Research (COSPAR), International Space Exploration Co-operation Group (ISECG) and International Astronomical Union (IAU) bring them together to co-operate on various domains annually or more frequently.

Within this busy multitude of fora, the Space20 can carve a niche for itself if it focuses on the wider aspects of "space economy" as it will be a natural extension of the G20's original global finance-economics purview. There is a lack of global understanding and consensus on the space economy, and UNOOSA, which has begun a capacity-building initiative around this domain, needs support from a strong multilateral body. Space20 can acquire this forte.

The G20 nations occupy the top echelons of global space activity. Very few nations outside this grouping are yet to develop comparable space competence. This capability gap can be filled if new economic mechanisms are promoted so that developing countries, from South America, Eastern Europe and Africa to Asia and Oceania, become part of technology supply chains, become recipients of cost-effective space services and be able to upgrade their environmental and socio-economic indicators by piggy-backing on the space-capable G20 nations.

India's growth story is exemplary among all the G20 countries. Our country's space programme has grown from the time India was considered a third-world economy to now being the third largest economy in the world. India has yet to grow on numerous socio-economic and environmental indices, but the path to future growth can happen if India can share its experiences and mentor countries from the developing world. With such antecedents, India will be an important player in the new Space20 group, and during its G20 Presidency in 2022, we should push a Space20 agenda championing the democratisation of outer space.

The largest democracy on the planet should promote democratisation of outer space by (a) lowering the barriers to enter the space industry by providing them access to cheap space-launch services, (b) offering superior space-based services – such as imaging and communications – cost-effectively and (c) enabling rule-abiding and responsible developing countries greater participation in the space economy. India has done all of this for several developing countries already. The South Asia Satellite being a prime technology example and the Dehradun-based UN Centre for Space Science and Technology Education in Asia and the Pacific being an institutional paragon.

The global space economy is poised to grow from the current $420 billion to $3.3 trillion by 2040.[32] Much of this growth will come from the commercialisation of space activities. India's recent privatisation of its national space sector is a step in this direction. Like India, many developing countries today have abundant natural and human resources that are necessary for the manufacturing of space and allied technologies.

These resources need to be engaged sustainably so that there is a tangible and quantifiable reduction in these nations' "distance to frontier" – a scoring mechanism that quantifies the gap between each economy's performance and the best practice and performance achieved by another economy across several economic and regulatory indicators. The higher the distance to frontier score, the higher the rankings on the ease of doing business. The Indian economy must aspire for the space economic frontier, by sharing its knowledge and best practices. The greater the shared knowledge, the more robust the practice, the shorter the distance to the frontier for the developing world. India is to only gain by sharing its knowledge.

To set a Space20 agenda on these lines, India must swiftly constitute an inter-ministerial Space20 working group that includes not only the space agency, ISRO, but also personnel from the new Indian National Space Promotion and Authorisation Centre (IN-SPACe) as well as experienced professionals involved in space policy, science, technology, economics and diplomacy.[33]

The year 2022 is also the momentous diamond jubilee of modern Indian state. It is the year when India looks back at its triumphs and failures with nostalgia and learning as well as views its future with high aspiration, confidence and intent to share knowledge. If India is to set an agenda of democratising outer space at the Space20 forum, it will be not only a big diplomatic endeavour but also a step towards making our country a global knowledge epicentre.

2.1.5 In the end, what did Riyadh achieve?

The Saudi-hosted Group of 20 (G20) summit on 21–22 November had an unusual backdrop.

U.S. President Donald Trump, defeated in the November 3 national election and delaying the presidential transition to his successor Joe Biden, prioritised improving his golf handicap over substantive participation in summit deliberations. Russian President Putin stood out in his refusal to congratulate President-elect Biden. Chinese President Xi Jinping and Prime Minister Narendra Modi had not talked in months, even as the two countries' troops continue a tense confrontation in eastern Ladakh.

These indicators of serious strains make the G20's claims about facing global challenges with solidarity and shared resolve, seem less credible. Yet, the world has no choice but to pay attention to what G20 does because it remains the most prominent forum for international cooperation.

Cutting through the rhetoric and wordy documents is necessary to correctly assess what G20 achieved during 2020, "this challenge-fraught year" as the Saudi King said. Crown Prince Mohammed bin Salman summed up the G20 commitments thus:

- $21 billion for tools and medicines to fight COVID-19,
- $11 trillion to support businesses and save jobs globally,
- $14 billion in debt relief to "the most vulnerable countries" under the G20's flagship programme – the DSSI,

- $300 billion raised by financial institutions to assist emerging and low-income countries.

This composite record sounds impressive but is not enough to overcome scepticism among critics and observers. Yet without the endeavours of the G20, the COVID-hit world may have been worse off. Therefore, what the G20 says and does is consequential. The virtual summit did have some achievements. The COVID shock and the trio of concerns – health, society, economy – was top of the agenda, with the group committing to mobilise resources for R&D, manufacturing and distribution of diagnostics, therapeutics and vaccines, to ensure full immunisation and "affordable and equitable access for all." A strategy to protect the global economy – the heart of the G20's existence – was reflected in the updated G20 Action Plan. It was much needed: as of November 2020, 46 countries requested to benefit from DSSI an estimated $5.7 billion in debt service deferral.

Beyond the immediate is the plan for a resilient and long-lasting recovery. These ranged from G20 actions to support world trade, treating infrastructure as a driver of growth to financial sector issues and international taxation. Support for WTO reform was articulated strongly, together with a recognition to increase "the sustainability and resilience" of national, regional and global supply chains. The Financial Stability Board was asked to continue "monitoring financial sector vulnerabilities" and enhance global cross-border payment arrangements. The digital economy received special attention, particularly issues concerning privacy, data protection, intellectual property rights and cyber security.

Besides, G20 remains committed to a whole spectrum of steps covered by its anti-money laundering and anti-terrorist financing policy as well as to strengthening the Financial Action Task Force's global network of regional bodies. The resolve to carry forward the global fight against corruption, including through "a multi-stakeholder approach," was stressed. This is an area with the clear imprint of Indian negotiators.

The arrival of potentially successful COVID vaccines gave the G20 both hope and caution. Even as the leaders endorsed the postponement of major public events as a way to mitigate the pandemic's impact, they commended Japan's determination to host the Olympics and UAE's resolve to host the World Expo in 2021.

And what of India? It swapped its G20 Presidency of 2022 with Indonesia in 2023 and will certainly be better prepared in physical, administrative and intellectual infrastructure. The new sequence of G20 chairs will be Italy (2021), Indonesia (2022), India (2023) and Brazil (2024). The latter three is a trio of developing countries, which must start coordination early to poise itself for an ambitious but implementable agenda, given the ever-rising expectations of the G20.

Recently, a former foreign secretary mentioned to this author that the world, beset with pressing challenges, needed "a missionary with a mission" but, instead, it had G20 as "a talk shop." John Kirton, professor at University of Toronto, assessed the Riyadh summit as "a small short-term success" for its resolve and decisions relating to the fight against COVID but faulted it for its failure to devise a "new coordinated stimulus" for revving up the global economy.

Prevailing fissures among the leading nations make it unrealistic to expect the G20 to deliver more. While operational level work proceeds, the top leaders should improve communication and trust among themselves. A sharper convergence in defining their national interests is essential. Perhaps the new president of the United States may help G20 do just that.

Notes

1 Johns Hopkins University. "Coronavirus Global Map." *Johns Hopkins University Coronavirus Centre.* 01 18, 2021. https://coronavirus.jhu.edu/map.html (accessed 01 18, 2021).
2 "Working Together to Defeat the COVID-19 Outbreak – Statement by Xi Jinping." *G20 Information Centre, University of Toronto.* 03 26, 2020. http://www.g20.utoronto.ca/2020/2020-g20-xi-0326.html (accessed 01 18, 2021).
3 University of Toronto. "Press Release on the Extraordinary Virtual G20 Leaders' Summit." *G20 Information Centre, University of Toronto.* 03 26, 2020. http://www.g20.utoronto.ca/2020/2020-g20-modi-0326.html (accessed 01 18, 2021).
4 "Remarks at the G20 Extraordinary Leaders' Summit on COVID-19 – Tedros Adhanom Ghebreyesus, Director General, World Health Organization." *G20 Information Centre, University of Toronto.* 03 26, 2020. http://www.g20.utoronto.ca/2020/2020-g20-tedros-0326.html (accessed 01 18, 2021).
5 Goodman, Matthew. "Assessing the G20 Virtual Summit." *CSIS.* 03 27, 2020. https://www.csis.org/analysis/assessing-g20-virtual-summit (accessed 01 18, 2021).
6 Johns Hopkins University. "Coronavirus Global Map." *Johns Hopkins University Coronavirus Centre.* 01 18, 2021. https://coronavirus.jhu.edu/map.html (accessed 01 18, 2021).
7 Stewart M. Patrick. "'The Multilateral System Still Cannot Get Its Act Together on COVID-19'." *Council on Foreign Relation.* 03 26, 2020. https://www.cfr.org/blog/multilateral-system-still-cannot-get-its-act-together-covid-19 (accessed 01 18, 2021).

8 "G20 Trade and Investment Ministerial Meeting: Ministerial Statement." *G20 Information Centre, University of Toronto.* 05 14, 2020. http://www.g20.utoronto.ca/2020/2020-g20-trade-0514.html (accessed 01 18, 2021).
9 "G20 Extraordinary Energy Ministers Meeting Statement." *G20 Information Centre, University of Toronto.* 04 10, 2020. http://www.g20.utoronto. ca/2020/2020-g20-energy-0410.html (accessed 01 18, 2021).
10 "Extraordinary G20 Digital Economy Ministerial Meeting: COVID-19 Response Statement." *G20 Information Centre, University of Toronto.* 04 30, 2020. http://www.g20.utoronto.ca/2020/2020-g20-digital-0430.html (accessed 01 18, 2021).
11 G20Information Centre, University of Toronto. *"Communiqué Virtual Meeting of the G20 Finance Ministers and Central Bank Governors." Riyadh, Saudi Arabia.* 04 15, 2020 (accessed 01 18, 2021).
12 G20Information Centre, University of Toronto. *"Communiqué Virtual Meeting of the G20 Finance Ministers and Central Bank Governors." Riyadh, Saudi Arabia.* 04 15, 2020. (accessed 01 18, 2021).
13 Chatzky, James McBride and Andrew. "The Group of Twenty'." *Council on Foreign Relations.* 06 10, 2019. https://www.cfr.org/backgrounder/ group-twenty (accessed 01 18, 2021).
14 These are: Business20, Think20, Civil20, Labour20, Science20, Womens20 and Urban20.
15 B20. " B20 Tokyo Summit Joint Recommendations "Society 5.0 for SDGs". B20 Tokyo 2019." B20 Japan. 03 15, 2019. http://www.keidanren. or.jp/en/policy/2019/020_Recommendations.pdf (accessed 01 18, 2021).
16 B20. "B20 Tokyo Summit Joint Recommendations "Society 5.0 for SDGs". B20 Tokyo 2019." B20 Japan. 03 15, 2019. http://www.keidanren.or.jp/en/ policy/2019/020_Recommendations.pdf (accessed 01 18, 2021).
17 B20. "B20 Tokyo Summit Joint Recommendations "Society 5.0 for SDGs". B20 Tokyo 2019." B20 Japan. 03 15, 2019. http://www.keidanren.or.jp/en/ policy/2019/020_Recommendations.pdf (accessed 01 18, 2021).
18 Johns Hopkins University. "Coronavirus Global Map." *Johns Hopkins University Coronavirus Centre.* 01 18, 2021. https://coronavirus.jhu.edu/ map.html (accessed 01 18, 2021).
19 Open letter to G20 Heads of State and Government', ICC and WHO." G20 Information Centre, University of Toronto. 03 23, 2020. http://www.g20. utoronto.ca/b20/2020-B20_WHO_and_ICC_joint_letter.pdf (accessed 01 18, 2021).
20 Al-Benyan, Yousef. "B20 Saudi Arabia, the Official Voice of the Private Sector to the G20, Welcomes the G20 Leaders' Commitment to Tackle the COVID-19 Pandemic." *B20 Saudi Arabia 2020.* 03 27, 2020. http://www. g20.utoronto.ca/b20/B20-welcomes-the-G20-Lea (accessed 01 18, 2021).
21 "'Joint Statement on Employment, Skills & Women', B20, L20, W20." G20 Information Centre, University of Toronto. 04 5, 2020. http://www.g20. utoronto.ca/b20/B20-L20-W20-final-statement-2020.pdf (accessed 01 18, 2021).
22 For backdrop, see Rajiv Bhatia, 'The Action Imperative for G20', Gateway House, 04 2, 2020. https://www.gatewayhouse.in/g20-action/ and Rajiv Bhatia, 'G20's role in the COVID-era', Gateway House, 21 May 2020, https://www.gatewayhouse.in/g20-covid-19/

23 Heger, Katrin and Downie, Richard, '. "Was the G20 Summit a "Win" for Africa?'." Centre for Strategic and International Studies. 07 27, 2017. https://www.csis.org/analysis/was-g20-summit-win-africa (accessed 01 18, 2021).
24 Floyd, Rob and Kapoor, Kapil. "G20 Compact with Africa." G20 Insights. 06 5, 2020. https://www.g20-insights.org/policy_briefs/g20-compact-with-africa/ (accessed 01 18, 2021).
25 Fabricius, Peter. "'G20 Compact with Africa Is a Long Game." Institute for Security Studies. 07 5, 2019. issafrica.org/iss-today/g20-compact-with-africa-is-a-long-game (accessed 01 18, 2021).
26 King of the Kingdom of Saudi Arabia. "Saudi King's Message to G20." *G20 Saudi Arabia.* 12 1, 2019. https://g20.org/Documents/Presidency-King-Message.pdf?v=1 (accessed 01 18, 2021).
27 Except to state that the Kingdom has 'a key role' to present "the perspectives of the Middle East and North Africa region, as well as the views of the developing countries."
28 "Virtual Meeting of the G20 Finance Ministers and Central Bank Governors." Communiqué. G20 Information Centre, University of Toronto. 07 18, 2020. http://www.g20.utoronto.ca/2020/2020-g20-finance-0718.html (accessed 01 18, 2021).
29 Arabia, G20 Saudi. "G20 Leader's Declaration. Saudi Arabia: G20, 2020." https://www.ilo.org/global/about-the-ilo/how-the-ilo-works/multilateral-system/g20/WCMS_761761/lang--en/index.htm
30 UNECA. "'ECA: Three Things the G20 Must Do to Support Africa in the COVID-19 Pandemic'." UNECA. 03 20, 2020. https://www.un.org/africarenewal/news/coronavirus/three-things-g20-must-do-support-africa-covid-19-pandemic (accessed 01 18, 2021).
31 Leininger, Julia and others. "G20 and Africa – Ready for a Steady Partnership." G20 Insights. 10 19, 2019. https://www.g20-insights.org/policy_briefs/g20-africa-ready-steady-partnership/ (accessed 01 18, 2021).
32 Giri, Chaitanya. "India Must Back Developing World in Space20." Gateway House. 10 26, 2020. https://www.gatewayhouse.in/india-space20/ (accessed 01 18, 2021).
33 Giri, Chaitanya. "India Must Back Developing World in Space20." Gateway House. 10 26, 2020. https://www.gatewayhouse.in/india-space20/ (accessed 01 18, 2021).

3 India in the G20
Through the T20 lens

3.1 Introduction

India's participation in the G20 has been enthusiastic, but limited. While the heads of government, finance ministers and central bank governors attended the G20 meetings, participation in the various sub-forums has been absent, as in the Think 20 (T20) or minimal even in critical groups like the Business 20.

In 2015, under the Turkish Presidency of the G20, for the first time, an Indian think tank, Gateway House, initiated and hosted a T20 meeting in India. It was in collaboration with TEPAV, the Turkish think tank assigned as the lead T20 sherpa, by Ankara. India's Central Bank governor, Dr. Raghuram Rajan, delivered the inaugural address – spelling out clearly what India's goal and journey for engagement with the global economy and its governance, should be. He who holds the pen, writes the rules, he said, and that should be India's goal, to move from being a passive global rule-taker, to being a confident global rule-maker.

Since then, every year, save 2020, Gateway House has hosted an annual T20 meeting in India, sometimes being the only country outside of the presidency country that a T20 meeting was held.

This chapter takes the reader through India's G20 journey, through the policymakers' speeches and interventions at the T20 meetings in India, to the speeches of its heads of government at the G20 summits and the Leaders' Declarations. These interventions show India's increasing confidence and desire not only to lead and direct the established themes of global financial regulation and trade but also to successfully engage on issues of particular relevance to India.

More specifically, these relate to terrorism financing, money laundering and transparency in financial flows worldwide; transparent cross-border flow of payments, remittances, aid and investments;

DOI: 10.4324/9781003152903-3

the high cost of remittances; identification of beneficial ownership in multi-country financial transactions to protect against money laundering, terrorist financing and tax evasion.

The broader global issues include reform of the Bretton Woods institutions, reconfiguration of global financial regulations, design of a new framework for the digital economy as also trade in services, establishing better cross-border standards for transparency in financial and participation in the new global commons – space, oceans, cyber.

3.2 India in the T20 Mumbai: what the policymakers say

2015
Raghuram Rajan
Oct 21, 2015.[1]

Dr. Raghuram Rajan, Governor, Reserve Bank of India, delivered the keynote address at India's first Think20 (T20) meeting organised by Gateway House with TEPAV, in Mumbai.

Global Economy and Challenges for Multilateral Policies

The agenda for the T20 is a vast one, so I have to pick and choose. I am going to focus today more on economic issues and leave aside the humanitarian, political and other issues.

I'm going to argue that world growth hasn't picked up ever since the crisis. And, in the G20 meetings recently as well as the IMF meetings in Lima, there's now talk of this – first the sub-prime crisis, then there was the European crisis, and now this talk of an emerging market crisis, or potential emerging market crisis.

And I'm going to argue these aren't three different crises; they are the same crisis happening in different ways. But the reason that this crisis is moving on from country to country, or region to region, is something that we have to be very worried about.

And there, there is scope for global action. It's difficult, but it may be necessary, if we have to get out of this regime of rolling crises – which I would argue didn't start with the global financial crisis, it actually started before, in the 1990s, with the emerging market crisis then.

Broadly speaking in the economic sphere, we need broad **new rules of the game** as well as a **reform of the multilateral institutions** to enforce them.

Is this going to happen in a hurry? No. That reflects some of the deficiencies in the multilateral discussion. But it's time to start talking and I would argue that some of the problems in global economic management are problems that you can see in the management of some of the other issues that were put on the table, and there are some similarities.

So with that as a description of what I'm going to talk about, let me jump into it. We've had fairly slow industrial country growth for the last seven years since 2008. And, there are various arguments for why this is the case. Of course, the first argument is we had a very deep crisis. Typically, you emerge from crises quite fast – recoveries from recessions are typically V-shaped. But, we haven't had much of a re-covery, let alone a V-shaped recovery.

One argument is this is because of the nature of the crisis. A lot of debt taken on – debt overhangs on corporations, on households make it very hard for them to borrow. Of course, most recently, governments have taken on debt – partly shifting debt from the corporations and households to their own balance sheets. Governments are also reach-ing the limits of their debt. So, one argument is – its debt.

And, we need the deleveraging, and the deleveraging is taking more time, and therefore, one shouldn't be too impatient. Of course, we did try to stimulate economies – the 2008 summit and subsequent summits were well known for the G20 urging countries to spend if they could. A number of countries took up the challenge of spending, and there were massive fiscal stimulus packages, including in our own country where we had three sequential stimulus packages.

These haven't done the trick – they haven't quite restored growth, including in our own country. There are arguments resurfacing today that the specifics of stimulus matter – we should build infrastructure. And, infrastructure is long-lasting, high returns, especially in times when construction material and construction costs are low because industries are underemployed – so let's build infrastructure. This was the mantra in industrial countries.

However, infrastructure investment took off only in a few countries and where it has taken off, it hasn't had much positive effect. Japan, for example. Massive infrastructure investments over the last couple of decades, but it still is not out of the woods. And part of the problem is, in many industrial countries, finding worthwhile infrastructure to build is hard. There's a lot of infrastructure already out there. Yes, everybody can see the potholes outside their window which needs fixing. Every-body can see a bridge or two that needs fixing. But beyond that, the large infrastructure projects, that would really move the needle on growth, are both harder to find, harder to coordinate on and harder to execute.

And, I think that the difficulties in the implementation of infra-structure in industrial countries aren't realised enough. In our own country, of course, we have massive infrastructure needs, and we're trying to go about them. But, infrastructure in industrial countries is more difficult.

So as people have found, that stimulus, whether monetary or fiscal, doesn't seem to be restoring growth. And even deleveraging – there's been a fair amount of deleveraging in the United States, some in Europe – even deleveraging doesn't seem to have restored growth, they've turned to the next possible reason why it hasn't happened. And, that's because structurally there were problems in the industrial countries which limited growth and we need to fix those structural problems.

Now what could be the structural problems? Most recently, a number of arguments that the nature of populations in industrial countries, ageing populations, have a different set of demands, a different set of supply possibilities and unless we cater to them specifically we are going to see growth slowdown as we have seen in Japan. That's one set of arguments.

Another set of arguments pertaining to what we heard just before I came on was on income inequality. Perhaps the movement of incomes towards higher-income people has, in fact, reduced overall demand. After all, poor people consume every rupee that they receive, but rich people – once you've bought your yacht and your private jet, there's not that much more you can spend on. And so the marginal propensity to consume out of incremental income is lower. That's the technical way of saying you don't have much to spend on when you're really rich. And so as a result, what you see perhaps is demand falling off.

So one argument is that we've had demand falling off for quite some time in industrial countries. It was boosted temporarily by the heavy debt that they took on pre-crisis, but post crisis with the high debt, it slowed down considerably. And so, we need to find ways of boosting demand, but it may be that it takes structural change, including, some people argue, shifting incomes from the richer to the poorer people. There have been arguments made along these lines.

Another set of arguments are about supply. The real problem is not demand, it's that we haven't had productivity growth in industrial countries, of the kind that would warrant sustained growth. And, the fairly low-productivity growth means that there can't be enough supply even if you generate the demand. And, of course, these two feed on each other. If you don't have productivity growth and you're unlikely to grow at a strong pace and create jobs, then people are more circumspect about spending and demand falls off. And similarly corporations, if they don't see productivity grow, if they don't see high profitability, are not going to invest so much – demand falls off. So, supply constraints or supply worries create a demand constraint, and similarly, if firms don't see enough demand, they don't actually invest. So, these things are highly interrelated, and you can't sort of separate one from the other.

But, the bottom line is that we need **structural reforms**. For example, if part of the problem is the elderly are going to move out of the workforce, and therefore, there are going to be supply constraints in the future, we need to find a way to get people who are not ordinarily participating in the labour force to come in. Which means that in countries like Japan, there's an argument that we should make it easier for women to come into the labour force – which means structural reforms on making it easier for women to work.

And you could argue that in Europe, the biggest constraint to growth is the low productivity in the service industry because of limited competition. The classic example is of the cartelised taxi industry and why don't we open it up. And organisations like Uber and so on are fighting to do that. But whether, in fact, there should be reforms which allow that to happen in a more serious way.

The problem with structural reforms as a pathway to growth is classically summarised by Jean Claude Junker who said – he was former Prime Minister of Luxembourg – "We all know what to do, we just don't know how to get re-elected after we've done it." So the problem with structural reforms is, they have the wrong timing of gain and pain. Politically what you want to do is something that has a lot of gain upfront and the pain is down the line because somebody else takes the blame for that.

But what happens is, with structural reforms, the pain is upfront because you are actually hitting the interests who benefit from the cosy system: the taxi drivers who have a cartelised system, by letting entrants in. The gain comes to the new entrants down the line, but they realise it only down the line after the reforms are done. And so the voters are going to compensate you five years from now, but then you're history by that time because the current taxi drivers have voted you out.

So the problem with structural reforms is, it's always fun to tell somebody else to do it, especially in other countries, but doing it in your own country is difficult. What we have is a real difficulty in generating growth. And it's a difficulty which is not just post-financial crisis, but I think pre-financial crisis, which, in fact, explains why we took on so much debt across the world pre-financial crisis, in an attempt to pump up growth, which just wasn't happening.

One possible answer is, grow slower – don't grow so fast and accept that **sustainable growth** – if you're not willing to do the structural reforms – is actually going to be at a lower rate. The problem is that it's very hard for governments to accept lower growth in the industrial world because the promises they made in times of high growth are coming back to roost. Entitlements in the 1960s on healthcare, on social security – certainly in the United States at the current trajectory – are un-payable. You cannot deliver on those promises; they are too big. But even since then, what has happened is, you have made more and more promises, often to public sector workers.

In the state that I know well because it's been a long time teaching at Chicago – Illinois, has made enormous promises to its public sector workers because it was always convenient. Harder to increase current wages because it will increase your budget but convenient to increase pensions because somebody else pays for it down the line while you get the credit. And so enormous pension promises, which simply cannot be delivered. So, you have all these entitlements coming, and then you have debt – debt taken on during the financial crisis, taken on before the financial crisis.

When you have all this, the only way to pay it is to grow. Growth is an imperative in many industrial countries. But it's not just growth for the sake of growth, it's the distribution of growth. That when you have a slowdown, the worst hit is the newcomers, the young. Because especially in societies which are more insider societies, the insiders are reasonably well protected, but it's the outsiders – the young, the immigrants who get hit. And, they can start raising their voice – the high levels of youth unemployment in Europe are a serious source of concern. But now, immigrant unemployment is contributing to that.

And of course, we talked about **inequality**. That's also an issue which has come to the forefront and it's not something to be dismissed lightly. It's one of the biggest forces governing political debate in industrial countries today. The fact that middle-class jobs are being lost – lost to technology, lost to global competition – means that a very strong constituency for stability is getting weaker and weaker. And again for the middle class, given that good middle class jobs are fairly small in number, you need growth to even create those additional jobs. So growth is absolutely an imperative.

And perhaps last, but more to the mind of central bankers – **deflation**. There is a very strong fear, especially in the United States, given its historical experience in the 1930s that if deflation takes hold, you will have a Japan-like experience and have to write off 15–20 years of growth. Now, I think that's a misreading of what happened in Japan, but nevertheless, there is a very strong fear amongst the central banking community across the world that deflation has to be averted at any cost. And, therefore, that's another reason to try and promote growth because if you have reasonable growth, you can avoid the deflation problem.

So, bottom line, to perhaps summarise quickly is – growth has been low, perhaps for decades we have masked it with a fair amount of debt and the current emerging market slowdown is just a reflection of the slowdown in industrial countries. If you think about the growth model that took off in the 1990s in the emerging markets – it was exporting to the industrial countries. And as the industrial countries slowed down, for a while the emerging markets concealed that slowdown with packages of their own – the massive debt-financed growth, for example, in China. But once they realised that the industrial country growth was going to be slow for a much longer time, the emerging markets also stepped down.

What we need in the world is obviously all these structural reforms that we are all reluctant to do. And so, we are all looking out for someone in the world to step up and grow faster and pull the world along. It used to be the United States that used to be this engine of growth, then perhaps some people look to China. But in this environment where nobody is willing to step up, there's a real question of how to give them a push. How do you push somebody to step up and pull us along?

This is where I think we enter dangerous territory, where the kind of method we give other people to push is through unconventional monetary policy. Including a shared rate intervention, which tends to push capital into other countries. As it pushes capital into other countries, it moves them a little faster for a while. But eventually this capital, where it moves the other country faster, creates difficulties for that country – we've seen this three times, and I'll come to that in a second.

That's what I meant by the crisis shifting from place to place. That we have in a sense, a **global game of musical crisis** and we have to worry about where this ends. Now how do you say this – where do you say this is from? I would say go back to the 1990s. In the early 1990s, interest rates were kept very low in industrial countries as countries including the United States were trying to revive their banks post the emerging market crises of the 1980s. So interest rates were low, capital flowed to the emerging markets. As the industrial countries revived and started raising interest rates, capital started flowing out. You have the Mexican crisis, you had the Asian financial crisis, you had the Argentinian crisis and nearly a Brazilian crisis – all in the span of three or four years, as capital flowed out because monetary policy tightened in industrial countries.

So what the emerging markets said is, never again, we're not going to be subject to this kind of thing, we're going to resist capital inflows. So every time capital comes in we are going to build up reserves. We had an enormous build-up of reserves in the emerging markets in the early 2000s. And because the capital from the emerging markets was now being pushed back to the industrial countries, some of the industrial countries started running large current account deficits. The United States – 6% at its peak, Spain, Greece, Portugal, all these countries. So think about which countries then got affected by crises.

It was now the turn of the industrial countries. The United States, then Spain, Greece, Portugal. And remember in 2005, Chairman Bernanke made his – he was still not Chairman at that point – but he made his famous savings glut speech, where he said the problem for the industrial countries, especially for the United States, was this flood of capital of savings coming from the emerging markets and distorting prices in industrial countries, and creating real estate booms, etc. So he complained about the capital flowing in and said we can't manage it.

That was a prescient speech and it preceded the U.S. financial crisis. Now think about what happened post-financial crisis. Post-financial crisis, the industrial countries slowed down tremendously. No more borrowing from the rest of the world to finance expansion. Fiscal deficits came down. And who now started becoming the next leg of the musical crisis – it was the emerging markets. Massive spending increases, including in India, which attracted a lot of capital, including in China, Turkey and Brazil. And that hasn't ended well either that all of us have slowed down considerably because we've had to manage the macro-economic consequences of absorbing serious amounts of capital. And now again as the prospect of interest rate start rising, starts taking hold, the capital is flowing out, leaving debris in its way.

Can we do this better than this? Where do we continuously push capital from one shore to another? Because the next leg of this is again a massive reserve build-up in the emerging markets as they try and deal with the consequences of capital flowing in. So, I would argue that what we have to worry about are policies that do this.

- That extreme monetary policies including both the exchange rate intervention that some of the emerging markets indulged in, in the early 2000s, as well as the unconventional monetary policies that the industrial countries have engaged in, had the primary effect of altering your exchange rate and pushing capital, and given that they are essentially creating problems for others, have large negative spillovers without the commensurate positive spillovers domestically.

- That if you have a policy which increases domestic growth enough and therefore allowed you to act as an engine of world growth that would be reasonable – that offsets any negative spillover effects that you might have. But if the primary effect is through the exchange rate, depreciating your currency, trying to sell goods to others while pushing capital to them, then, in fact, you could argue, you're not playing the appropriate role as global citizen – you're having more effects outside than inside.

Unfortunately, if you look at central banking mandates across the world, no central bank has a mandate for the world. Its mandate is purely domestic – what are you going to do to elevate employment and growth. It has to worry about the world only at a second level. If I do something which creates problems for another country, and as a result demand from that country falls off for my country's goods, I should take that into account, the feedback effects. But not the feed-forward – I don't care if I destroy that other country completely, so long as it doesn't import from me. I'm okay, right? That kind of domestic mandate is actually there in every country. This is not pointing fingers at any central bank.

We haven't got mandates for the world. And as a result monetary policy even in its most aggressive kind – and I want to put an equivalence between unconventional monetary policy and direct exchange rate intervention because sometimes they have the same effect – and I want to argue that we're in a world where there's nothing that prevents these kinds of policies. There's nobody looking at them. The IMF is supposed to look at these things in a global sense. But the IMF has been sitting on the side lines applauding these kinds of policies right from when they were initiated and hasn't really questioned the value of these kinds of policies. Yes, it does spillover studies. But the spillover studies invariably say this is good for their country and, therefore, good for their world. I think we need to examine these issues again.

So bottom line, can we do better? Yes, we can do better. Of course, the world needs more investment and that means in the emerging markets that have the need for infrastructure investment, such as ours, we need to do much more investment. We certainly are prepared to do it, we have large plans and we are beginning to do them – the Delhi-Mumbai Industrial Corridor, the Eastern and the Western freight corridors. Lots of plans and we are embarked on it.

But emerging markets embarking on infrastructure also need support. There is now a view that multilateral institutions don't need to provide finance, all they need to do is provide advice because the private markets can do the rest. Private markets can do a lot. But private markets are not often the best source of patient risk capital. And sometimes patient risk capital with knowledge is what the multilateral institutions provide. At a time when the world needs infrastructure, shrinking the multilateral institutions is not a great idea. And the fact that there is space here is a reason why we have all these new institutions coming up. Ideally, India has always stood for global engagement, global multilateralism – we want the existing multilateral institutions to be strengthened, not weakened.

From the industrial country perspective, there certainly is scope for investment, but it may not be the typical infrastructure, it may be green infrastructure. We know that the world has to deal with climate change and environmental issues sooner rather than later. Perhaps the onus of the investment to deal with that has to come from the industrial countries, which have a much greater responsibility for the current levels of carbon in the atmosphere. So an emphasis on green in the industrial countries. And of course, we have our part to play, the emerging markets, and we will.

But an emphasis on replacing, in the existing stock of investment which is non-green, to investment which is green, is something the industrial countries can do much more of, it's a clear need, it is something that can be revived at this point. And I think the countries that are emphasising this, such as Germany, Japan and, to some extent, the United States, are going down the right path.

We need new rules of the game on policy. And I think we always retreat as central bankers to say we have a domestic mandate. What we need is a political consensus to go beyond domestic mandates to think in this integrated world where monetary policies affect each other, what might be a sensible way of moving forward. I don't want to pose any easy solutions to this – happy to discuss it in a debate, but it is something that we need to do.

Now even while I say we need a better cohesion, better coordination on at least mandates, I would also say that we have to be very careful in this world, in avoiding financial repression.

Let me explain. Even when I say impatient capital flows easily across borders, every country today needs patient capital. In the industrial countries, it's about financing the long-term pensions that are going to be due in financing the debt of governments. And similarly, in the emerging markets, its financing long-term infrastructure. One worry is that with the spate of new regulations that are coming up in the financial sector that it tends to be biased against long-term patient flows in the emerging market because long-term flows have a much higher risk weight and flows to emerging markets which are lower weight than industrial countries also have a very high risk rate.

So as we are getting stronger and stronger regulations in the financial sector, it may have the effect of chilling the needed flows, even while the less needed flows are encouraged relatively because they're short term, invested in government security, etc. and can be put in at a moment's notice. So the worry is long-term patient capital should not be repressed by the kinds of global regulations that we're getting in so that capital which is needed in the emerging markets sit in the industrial countries and doesn't move, while the un-needed or less-needed capital flows more effectively.

Given that we have these capital flows – and certainly it's very hard to separate the good from the bad – we probably also need better global safety nets to ensure that those who accept this capital and who use it have liquidity protection in case the capital wants to run out. Typically, the IMF is supposed to do this kind of activity but unfortunately because of past history, certainly in Asia but, to some extent, in Latin America, there's an enormous stigma in going to the IMF, which is why countries in the region are developing regional arrangements rather than going to the multilateral institutions. For example, we have lent a billion and a half dollars to Sri Lanka as part of a swap arrangement we have with them. But better than this would be a stronger multilateral global safety net and we need to work towards making that possible. It would be needed because going directly to the IMF carries an enormous stigma and very few countries in Asia are willing to do that.

Of course, the concern amongst a number of countries that would put out the money is moral hazard. If we make money too easy, lots of countries will do things that are not appropriate, get into trouble and then call for funding. But there has to be a way to balance these two interests and we need to find out a way to make these global safety nets up and running; otherwise, there will be countries that would be left out and not in any kind of succour when, in fact, the global financial conditions change.

One proposal that has been put out which deserves examination is central bank swap lines mediated and backed up by the Fund. There are some proposals like this floating, but at this point, we need political support for something like this because central banks simply don't have the capability of agreeing to this on their own.

Finally, we need better legitimacy for the global multilateral institutions. This is not just about quotas which are held up say for the IMF. This is not just about who appoints the managing director or where the managing director comes from. This is more about having a more inclusive discussion. Which means one, the agendas that are proposed, for what we work on, have to be more inclusive and reflect the interests of the developing countries and emerging markets also.

It cannot be just driven by what is important on the industrial country plate. The staff of these institutions typically tend to have a world view which is driven by where the institution is located and where they hire from. Doesn't matter that they have citizens from all countries – if the citizens have all been to the same kinds of institutions in the industrial world and then live in Washington or Frankfurt or somewhere else, they tend to have a world view which is driven by that location. And that also makes it much harder for them to appreciate what is happening elsewhere. So, we need to think about how we deal with that issue also.

But finally I think, and this is where I will come back to the T20, we need more capacity in the emerging markets. I say propose agendas – well the industrial countries will push back and say you can propose an agenda anytime you want. We don't do it. We don't do it often because we haven't thought enough. We haven't developed our own capacity to provide new ideas to the global financial system. So we're almost always in reactive mode – "What did they say? Do we like it or do we not?" instead of saying "Here's what we say." For the first time with the new institutions that are being proposed, largely by China, we're starting to put some new alternatives on the table. But we must, across the emerging world, realise that some of the reasons why global governance seems to be sort of against us are we're not putting enough resources into this.

Let me give you just one example. The G20 framework working group is supposed to be co-chaired by Canada and India. So it's a fair arrangement, an emerging market with an industrial country. But Canada has seven strong economists working on this group, trying to further the agenda, while India brings far fewer people to the table. Because we don't have that strength in the number of economists who can actually contribute. Yes, we go to our think tanks, etc., but we don't have people working in government who have that kind of training and that kind of a capacity. And as a result, what happens is more of the pen and the writing is done by the Canadians. And they've stepped up to the plate – this is a natural consequence.

But it would be far better for us to bring more people to the working group so that we act as equal partners, rather than let them do the writing while we do the commenting. In fact, when I was co-chair of that working group we actually wrote a few and it turned out that it makes a big difference who has the pen. Because what you write is very different – and actually we did the first piece on spillovers. In February 2013, before the taper tantrum, saying this is something we need to start worrying about as industrial country market policies normalise. And it was something that at least shone the spotlight on something we needed to talk about and was very important.

So bottom-line, a lot of demand for growth. The policies that add to global growth could be far better and perhaps there's a reason to coordinate because countries are indulging more in policies that shift growth from others to themselves rather than create more growth for the global economy. So, while staying away from the protectionism. That's a benefit of the global economy today. We may have strayed into comparative easing and that's a concern. We do need to look at globally optimal policies and for that, I think we need to focus on how we improve global institutions. And I think this forum is a very good start. Thank you.

2016:
Dr. Arvind Panagariya
13 June 2016.[2]
Arvind Panagariya, G20 Sherpa, Government of India, delivered the keynote address at the 2016 T20 Mumbai meeting hosted by Gateway House
China, India and the G20
Discussing China's priorities for G20 in 2016 and India's contributions to the G20 agenda
Director, Gateway House, Neelam Deo, Mr. Jin Song, Professor Zhibo, distinguished guests and friends. Let me first express my deep sorrow at the loss of 50 innocent lives yesterday in Orlando, Florida in the United States. After a very uplifting visit by the Prime Minister, this was a bit of dampening news last night.

The subject today is the G20. And at T20, let me first begin by congratulating our guests from China here who have done a superb job of organising this year's presidency. We already have had two Sherpa meetings and, of course, there are dozens and dozens of other meetings that are going on, and I can testify first-hand that the arrangements in all their aspects have been absolutely unmatched.

As you all know, G20 is the premier global economic governance platform. It consists of 20 members, obviously, but the twist is that there are 19 countries which are members, but the 20th one is the European Union representative. The countries that are members (these are the numbers given out generally) account for about 85% of the gross world output and 75% of world trade, not counting the EU intra-trade. If you count EU intra-trade, it's about 80% of the world trade.

Roughly, all the major countries are members – the United States, Canada, from North America, Mexico, from Latin America (I won't say North America, although Mexico sort of goes into the Latin America basket) and then we got Japan, the large members of the original European Economic Community, (Germany, France, Italy, Turkey), the five BRICS countries we say four, but I think South Africa, Brazil, Russia, India, China, South Africa, Indonesia, South Korea, Mexico, Australia, Argentina, Saudi Arabia and as I said, the European Union. The presidency can also bring in special invitees, typically these are countries but they can also bring in international organisations as special invitees. Several of the international organisations are regular invitees and they sit through the meetings.

There are two tracks – Neelam mentioned those. There is the finals track – where it all really started – and there is what Neelam called the development track, we more loosely call it the Sherpa track which is where I participate and represent India. In the finance track year, you have the Finance Ministers and Central Bank Governors' meeting. It was originally conceived in 1999. At that time, it was the Finance Minister's Forum, but after the 2008 global financial crisis, it then was converted into the Heads of States meetings.

The Sherpa track or the development track meets four times a year – of which one happens to be the summit. Usually, the summit meeting is the last run. This time, rather unusually, because the summit is happening earlier in the year, in September, they're actually going to bring it even further forward because Germany, the next presidency, has elections somewhere in July or so. So next year, it's going to be even earlier. So as a result, the first three meetings will be followed by the summit this year and there will be the fourth meeting after the summit – this is a bit unusual.

There are also ministerial meetings that take place. We got agriculture, energy, commerce and labour. So the various ministers from the G20 countries meet to negotiate on these specific areas. And then, of course, we've got the groups – T20, this is a think tank 20, which is where we are today, B20, (Business 20), W20, the Women's Group which Turkey started last year and so forth.

One of the first questions that was posed to me was "beyond 2008, what relevance will G20 have today?" Of course you know so the crisis really – the "crisis" crisis – is over, but the aftermath of the crisis remains with us. Global growth certainly has not picked up and so that issue still remains with us. You know this was a big issue in Brisbane and the commitment was made that the countries will take – each member country will take – actions which will together raise the level of GDP by an extra 2% points by 2018. So a lot of countries kind of submitted their country action plans, but that's just an example.

The agenda of the G20 remains quite wide so let me just try to give you a bit of a list. It's not just about – although global crisis is what really led to the upgrading of the G20 to the leader's summit level – the issues are not limited only to the crises. Growth, as I mentioned – that's always an ongoing issue – but a number of other issues which relate to the global economic governance (some maybe even transcending economic governance although generally with some sort of implications for the economic side as well) do come to G20.

So you got growth, as I mentioned. Then, climate change is a major issue which remains a recurring theme of discussion at the G20 meetings. Trade remains at the centre. Again, these are issues of global economic governance. Energy, that is another important issue, and anti-corruption where India has been at the forefront, is also an issue. Food security and employment, yet new issues get added. I'll also talk a little bit about that as I speak about what is going on under the current Chinese Presidency.

But some new issues that have now been added to the agenda include the sustainable development goals, investment issues, refugee crisis, global health – in particular, the entry of microbial-resistance – counterterrorism, finance, etc. So it's a very wide agenda and when we go for the meetings for two days we are, in fact, very, very busy. We are kept pretty intensely engaged and occupied.

One further question that was given to me was whether G20 is being run by the G7. That is a question about whether the developing countries are largely running the show at G20. Let me assure you not. So by a long shot, G7, G20 countries are as tough negotiators as any; G7 countries play a very crucial role in steering the non-G7 positions.

We negotiate very intensely, and not all issues necessarily put us into confrontational situations. Nevertheless, there are nuances to every issue which can cut across developed and developing countries and we do negotiate tough. What I found personally – I think my personal experience during four or five of these meetings that I've attended – is that the very good thing about this forum is it's a very congenial forum. It's a very friendly forum, where I particularly, – to me since I've been a professor for most of my life – the very refreshing thing is to find out that good arguments find lots of traction regardless of who makes them.

That really is a very fulfilling experience.

Give and take works. If you are always wanting and not willing to give, then life gets tough. You can't get concessions if you're not willing to give concessions. One has to be somewhat in that spirit – one can negotiate tough, but at the end of the day, if you are simply not offering anything, it is very unlikely that you are going to get anything. That was the first lesson I learned at the first sherpa meeting that I attended. And I was very happily surprised that when I gave a concession on an issue on which I could give a concession, I very quickly was rewarded with something in return. That is the spirit with which we negotiate. The Prime Minister has been, in that respect, very encouraging. We should not be obstructionist as often as we are accused of doing. And so I think we do, and I'll give you lots of examples as I go forward and describe some of the experiences. The key lesson that I have learned is that if in a negotiation, you have to confine your negotiation within the negotiating space. Sometimes if you really want to ask for concessions that are outside of the negotiating space, then that gets a bit tougher.

Next issue was about the Chinese Presidency. I've already mentioned my general comment that this has been an extremely well-run show. Sure enough, China is setting a very tough example for India, – a very high standard for India – because remember that in either 2018 or 2019, India would be the host for G20 so we'll be the presidency then. It is still not clear whether it's going to be 18, or 19 but certainly one of those two years. China has sought to give a new direction to ongoing issues while also placing new issues on the table.

So, for example, growth is an ongoing issue, but here China has given a new direction to it. China has brought in issues that were not part of the discussion on growth previously. In particular, China has focused on three new areas – digital economy, innovation and a new industrial revolution. That is now on the centre stage of the discussion. It really sits very well for China because that is where China is heading. But, it also sits very well for India because that is where India has some strengths. That is also an issue for the global economy because we are all now moving towards a much more innovation-driven digital economy with a new industrial revolution likely to be happening in the next coming few decades. Among the new issues, as an example, you got the Sustainable Development Goals, these were negotiated in the United Nations but have now been brought centrally also into the G20 discussions by China.

China has also put the investment issue on the table. This was not a part of the discussions before, in particular. This really speaks to where China currently sits, so it's a bit between the developing and the developed that China is not only now the recipient of large foreign investment, but it is also investing abroad just as India is too, but China perhaps much more so. And, therefore, it is a natural thing for China to want to then lay down the work, the foundation for possibly new rules on investment as we go forward. So, this is a major issue that has emerged under the Chinese Presidency.

Then, there are also issues that do not necessarily get driven by the presidency but by other members. Global health in the context of the antibiotics is one such issue. We also try to avoid duplication and therefore the sustainable development goals are on the G20 agenda, but it is not in the same sense that it is on the agenda of the United Nations. What we try to do is focus on where the collective action matter is, –where, therefore, the G20 can add some value to the subject. So things like infrastructure, finance, food security and nutrition, remittances, international tax cooperation, energy, trade – these are the areas in which collective action can help promote the SDGs so that's what the presidency is focusing on. So that's some rough labour for what is happening currently in the Chinese Presidency.

Briefly let me speak to the role of India and this is where I can perhaps tell you a little from personal experience. Also perhaps that can highlight a little bit on the role the non-G7 countries play in the G20. So, we have certainly played a very critical role for articulating the interests of emerging market economies in the G20 discussions. I have excellent working relations with South Africa, Turkey, Saudi Arabia and Indonesia. We also have great partnership with Argentina – this was particularly true, and this great partnership worked out with Argentina during the Antalya summit. We worked very closely and that as I will describe briefly, turned out to be extremely fruitful.

We also work with Brazil, China and Russia, – there is a subgroup within the G20 called the "Emerging Market Economies" which these countries are members of. Turkey has joined as the member of that subgroup as well. We don't always agree necessarily on every issue, but issue wise, wherever we see the scope for partnership, we try to do that. And that is also true in some of the cases with the other countries, including sometimes Japan –like on clean coal. We could have some partnership with Japan, so the views that we air at the meetings are often echoed back by other countries at the Sherpa meetings. Let me get to a few details.

The Antalya leaders' communiqué, which I negotiated on behalf of India, had India's stamp everywhere. I'll tell you a few details. The developed countries had demanded much stronger and also sort of assisted by the ILO, very strong language on the harmful effects of inequality on growth. And I sort of felt that overemphasis on that then can have adverse implications for what you would do for growth. That can, in an odd sort of way, lead you to actually take steps by which you would compromise growth. So, I strongly argued and based on very empirical evidence – if you know the empirical evidence, then it's harder for the other side to push you – that the relationship between equality and growth was weaker. So, the language that went into the communiqué was somewhat weaker than what the developed countries had pushed for.

International Labour Mobility – there was a gain in efforts by some of the countries to keep reference to international mobility out of the communiqué I insisted and some countries supported us so international labour mobility was very much a part of the communiqué.

There were also references to a new acronym called LIDC (low-income developing countries). The way LIDC is defined is such that India and Indonesia, who are members of G20, are not counted among LIDCs. And I feel very strongly on any of the trade issues we already had a different terminology – the least developed countries and the developing countries – and so you cannot start using a different classification to define trading rights of the countries. So far, for example, we have the special differential treatment provisions in the WTO – they apply to the developing and the least developed countries and that is how it should remain. So we ensured that when references to LIDCs are made, they are made not in the context of trade issues. So that also went in.

The United States had pitched very much that the references to the Doha Development Agenda not be included in the communiqué. We had insisted that the references ought to be there. So very pointed references to the world development agenda did remain in the communiqué. On energy, the United States had pushed very hard that we adopt some sort of medium-term deadline to end all the fossil fuel subsidies. While India has seen huge progress on fossil fuel subsidies having deregulated the price of both diesel and petrol and in other areas, coal cess, etc., made lots of progress in cutting subsidies on fossil fuels, nevertheless, we know that our states subsidise farmers on electricity and also on fertilizers. So we really were not in a position to accept a deadline and that deadline was, therefore, kept out.

I think the toughest negotiation I had in Antalya was on climate change. This was a negotiation on – leave aside all the other issues – climate change which on its own took two very long nights. On the first night, we negotiated for almost nine hours and could not come to an agreement. And at the end what was then, therefore, put out that was in a way for the Sherpa track the last day of negotiations. Finally, the

Turkish Presidency decided to put a particular weak paragraphed one which there was no difference, but the next day actually many of the leaders, particularly the developed countries objected to that. Therefore, the Sherpas went to work again that time. So there was the first day of the summit itself when around 10 o'clock at night, we went back to work and that negotiation went all the way till 4 o'clock.

The difference was that France, in particular, supported by the United States, the United Kingdom, etc. and was very keen to achieve some or cross some of the hurdles that had to be crossed in Paris where the actual negotiation on climate change was due to happen. France wanted to tie up some of those issues in Antalya. I was of the view that there's a negotiation to happen in Paris, so it was a very torturous negotiation, but in the end, we successfully maintained the status quo.

So when our negotiators arrived in Paris, they arrived without their hands tied in any way. It gave them greater negotiating space, so perhaps the most satisfying thing in all this is that although we did negotiate quite tough, the end of the day, we did it in a very congenial manner, giving our arguments and at the end, therefore, you heard not a single nation accuse us of being obstructionists. So I think this was a change for the better from what we had experienced in the past.

Lastly, let me take one or two more minutes, I was asked what the T20 can do. Let me say that a lot of the intellectual work for the G20 is done by the international organisations. These include particularly the Organisation for Economic Co-operation and Development (OECD), the foremost, I think tends to be most active, the World Bank, International Monetary Fund, Financial Stability Board (FSB), WTO and ILO – these are the main ones. Right now China has also invited UN-IDO, I think? United Nations, of course, also sits there. Many of these international organisations are more attuned to the issues that are of interest to the developed countries, therefore, to the G7. And I think really this is where the T20 could fill a major gap – to look at the issues that are of interest to the developing countries so, therefore, help identify what positive demands can countries like India and China make at the negotiating table.

We are still, I would say on balance – a lot of the negotiating issues actually get put by the developing countries. We then react. It is changing. We have been putting some of our own issues like we talked about the remittances, international labour mobility, etc. So we have tried to bring issues of interest to the developing countries to the table. Still more issues come from the G7 countries. And I think if you're going in a negotiation and simply react, that's no good, this is where it is very important to identify what we want out of a negotiation.

And I think this is where the T20 can really be helpful. Specifically, let me say that in 2018 or 2019, India will be hosting and, therefore, the natural question is what ought to be India's agenda for the G20 Presidency. I think that is where you could actually do a lot of work, help us. If I'm still serving as the Sherpa, I would be delighted to get that help.

Thank you again, for inviting me. It has been a pleasure.

2017
Yonov Frederick Agah
13 February 2017[3]
Yonov Frederick Agah, the Deputy Director, World Trade Organisation, delivered the keynote address at the 2017 T20 Mumbai meeting hosted by Gateway House

Your Excellencies, Distinguished panellists, I wish to express my sincere thanks to the co-hosts, the Indian Council on Global Relations and the Kiel institute on World Economy for the privilege of speaking at this distinguished and timely panel on how and where the G20 can help build consensus on issues of critical importance.

Coming from the WTO, you can guess my answer, which is quite short and straight forward. Nothing is more important for developing countries today than the maintenance of the multilateral trading system. Developing countries are the fastest rising trade powers and their economies are the most dependent on global trade. They are the most reliant on the rules of the multilateral trading system, to keep world markets open and to level the playing field. The science of global trade among protectionist sentiments should be deeply worrying to say the least for developing countries.

Under these circumstances, the G20 members can help the global consensus by enforcing actions as well as words and can ensure a fair commitment to the open world trading system, aided by a strong and effective WTO.

The fastest-growing trade powers today are not the advanced power of Europe and North America, even though they are critical, they are the developing countries of Asia, Africa and South America. The developing world's share of global trade has grown from less than a third in 1980 to nearly half today and our current trends, the share is likely to continue to grow in the foreseeable future. China, to take the most obvious example, is now the world's largest exporter, while it was a mere 32nd in 1980. While countries like China and India have captured the lion's share of the world's attention, the story of the developing world's rapid trade rise includes countries of all sizes and regions – Vietnam, Cambodia and Madagascar have seen their exports surge since 2010, and their relative debts far exceed the numbers of Brazil and China.

With their growing integration into the global economy, developing countries' reliance on trade – import and export – continues to rise. Trade now accounts for over 35% of developing countries' economic output on average, compared to 25% of advanced countries, making them the most trade-dependent economies. This is not only because the multilateral trading system has become more open but also because developing countries have dramatically lowered their import barriers. In an era when two-thirds of world trade now takes place within global production networks and developing countries ability to increase exports is directly dependent on their ability to receive imports, an open and stable connection to the world markets is very essential, and this is only not just for increasing trade but also for attracting foreign investment, technology and other factors of production that are critical for the continued growth and development of developing countries.

As developing countries share of and dependence on the world trade has grown, so has their reliance on the trading system. In the GATT era of industrial economies, the industrialised economies largely dominated the system. Today, the emerging economies like India, China and Brazil play a role that was unimaginable 20 years ago. Dozens of the developing countries are today contributing actively and constructively to a system that they have a big stake. The biggest change is also in mindsets. More and more developing countries have come to see increased trade, more open markets and a stronger WTO as core development issues devoted to their development progress and they are relying less on protectionism as a development strategy. Not only because it punishes their citizens by inflating the prices for necessities like food, energy and clothing but also because it handicaps their industries. They cannot hope to compete in global markets without access to world-class inputs, investments and technology. It is, therefore, no coincidence that the 2030 sustainable development goals highlight the need to significantly increase the exports of developing countries and promote a universal, rules-based and non-discriminatory multilateral trading system.

Trade is the only condition for development today. It is not only just a condition; it is a necessary one, which explains why outward-oriented developing countries are also making great strides in health, legal standard and poverty reduction. Let me clear, the developing world's economic progress hinges on maintaining a stable world trading system. Developing countries need a stronger rules-based trading system, not weaker ones, more trade liberalisation, not less and more global policy cooperation, not more isolation in bilateral or regional blocs.

While regional agreements can complement the multilateral trading system, they cannot substitute for it. By design, they are discriminatory and exclusive, risking the direction of trade and investment and marginalise those left outside. They can create overlapping and inconsistent rules, thereby increasing trade costs, increasing complexity and adding weakness. They tend to increase the leverage of the stronger trade powers at the expense of the smaller ones. This is why many developing countries should approach this with caution.

Since regional agreements lack the global cooperation and scope of the WTO, they are inherently limited in their ability to address growing global trade challenges from disciplining subsidies to regulating digital trade. This is why a strong emphasis of this year's German G20 Presidency, like last year's Chinese Presidency on issues like further liberalising trade, reducing industrial tariffs and tackling non-tariff barriers remain of central importance to developing countries. Likewise digital trade, services liberalisation and investment consultation remain key priorities of the German presidencies and are important developmental issues.

Indeed, the distinction between developing and advanced countries negotiating issues is becoming narrower if not blurred. In the light of the developing world's rise to trade prominence and their need for coherent approaches across numerous policy areas, including global integration – development is now a core objective and an inherent part of everything that the WTO does. I do not need to remind this distinguished audience about the major challenges this system now faces and the costs of complacency.

2016 marked a fifth consecutive year with weak trade growth below 3%, a situation seen only once in the past 70 years. Weak growth in major economies and weak investment in multipolarity has played a key role. So too has the slowing pace of global trade liberalisation, coupled with the steady accumulation of protectionist measures. The latest of the G20-WTO monetary report shows that the number of trade-restrictive measures remains high, and a starting commitment by the G20 remains slow. The report warns that the G20 economies must focus their efforts and resolve this. It is true that anti-trade and anti-globalisation sentiments seem to be gaining traction, especially in several key advanced countries. This is one of the main issues discussed by leaders at the recent G20 summit and is a key agenda item of the Trade and Investment Working Group under the German Presidency.

The WTO, IMF and World Bank are working on a discussion paper that shows benefits that will flow from further trade integration. The paper will also highlight that there is no gain in terms of better jobs and higher growth without the pain of structural transformation and diversification, as capital and labour are reallocated across sectors.

Let me, therefore, conclude with the observation that in today's hyper-connected, multipolar trading economy, the multilateral trading system is becoming more and more and not less important to the developing countries. This also means that the costs of failure are higher and the ramifications of it will be felt more widely. We must continue to make a case for global trade and the multilateral trading system, as it will otherwise open the door to a rather uncertain future. This is where the consensus building work done by G20 bodies at Gateway and the Kiel Institute is so critical. This reminds us that today's multilateral trading system grew out of the world's disaster in the 1930s, from protectionism and devastation from wars. It was the power of an idea that global peace can only be achieved from shared global prosperity and development, which means global development in today's order. I share the view that we forget those lessons at our own peril. Distinguished ladies and Gentlemen, I thank you for your kind attention.

2018
Shaktikanta Das
12 March 2018[4]
Shaktikanta Das, G20 Sherpa for India, gave an interview on the side-lines of the 2018 T20 meeting in Mumbai. Excerpts from the interview are below.

India has always cooperated with G20 presidencies to foster consensus on various issues. All three priorities that the Argentine Presidency has raised are very relevant for India.

The first is the future of work or employment in the context of robotics, automation and Artificial Intelligence (AI). As you know, various groups in India are working on AI. While it can be a threat to some jobs in the short term, in the long run, it can create new employment opportunities. So, it is a priority for India.

Infrastructure for development is again very important. Infrastructure investment provides great momentum for growth. India has placed disaster-resilient infrastructure on the agenda. This was addressed by our honourable prime minister during the Hamburg Summit in 2017, and we want to focus on it to improve the life cycle cost of infrastructure.

The future of food is very important for India because we need sustainable soil health and sustainable agriculture to have enough food production for a growing global population.

The three priorities for the Argentine Presidency are clearly India's too, and there is much convergence in our approach and theirs.

Our prime minister has been placing on the table issues of global importance, whether combating terrorism, fighting corruption or dealing with climate change. With Japan, which is our strategic partner, India will continue to play an important role. I think issues involving development and trade will be important. India will continue to extend its full support and cooperation to the Japanese leadership.

India has been an important voice in the G20 deliberations. It will continue to promote inclusive development, fairness in world trade, efforts to address malnutrition and hunger and poverty reduction. So India will play an important role just as it has been doing all along.

2019
A. Gitesh Sarma, Secretary28 January 2019.[5]
B. Gitesh Sarma, Secretary, Ministry of External Affairs, Government of India, delivered the keynote at the 2019 Think20 Mumbai Roundtable

Right at the outset, let me commend Gateway House for bringing us together in this way. Let us recall that G20 emerged in 1999 as a Forum of Finance Ministers and Central Bank Governors. And already by 2008, it had been elevated to the level of heads of state and government. Interestingly, Gateway House was established in 2009. In these ten years, it has become a most credible think tank, and everyone looks forward to the results of its deliberations.

Last night, we met informally, and I was recalling that it is not by accident that we meet in Mumbai. This is India's commercial capital, financial hub and home to Bollywood. This is the city of dreams, and also the city where dreams are turned into reality – provided we work hard. But sadly, this city is also one that has seen tragedy and reminds us how vulnerable we are to forces of evil – unless we join hands to create a better world. In fact, it is this very venue that reminds us of this lesson.

Friends, since its inception in 2012, this forum has helped the G20 arrive at concrete policy measures and its contribution must be commended. The deliberations of T20 feed into the deliberations of G20. Let us remember that G20 together contributes around 85% of global GDP, over 75% of global trade and is home to two-thirds of the world's population.

There is the expectation that G20 would focus on the most topical issues of the day facing mankind, as a whole, and help in setting

the global agenda. This becomes especially important when we find that global institutions, like the United Nations Security Council, World Bank and IMF, do not adequately reflect contemporary realities.

I commend Japanese think tanks and institutions and Gateway House for joining hands to organise this important meeting. The friendship between India and Japan has a long history, rooted in spiritual affinity and very strong cultural and civilisational ties. Today, India is the fastest growing, major economy, and Japan, one of the most advanced economies of the world: this is really a dream partnership and we are working together to take this relationship to a new level. The relationship has already been upgraded to "Special Strategic and Global Partnership."

At the start of 2019, the global economic outlook continues to be subdued. There are challenges coming from increasing protectionism and policy uncertainties, disorderly financial market movements, slow-productivity growth, skill deficiencies in emerging economies, the implementation of unsustainable macroeconomic policies and a host of other factors.

At the same time, we have to deal with more fundamental shifts. The reality is that the world is at the crossroads of transition today, given the rapid changes in technologies, Artificial Intelligence and the digital revolution. The socio-economic landscape of the future will be determined by how we respond to this transformation.

Demographic shifts, changing character of production and employment and technology-induced transformations are altering the way we do things. The digital revolution has fundamentally blurred the lines between the physical, digital and biological worlds. I myself recall how about 20 years ago, when the internet came, and the way it came, we spoke of the death of distance itself.

These changes are both challenges and opportunities, for people and governments. It has also taken us into uncharted territories for policy making and coordination, including in the international arena. The time has come to focus on inclusive growth in both national and international contexts.

Another key challenge is that the benefits of globalisation have not spread evenly. This has resulted in mistrust and opposition to globalisation, social tensions and a rise in expectations, which limit space for governments. There are also heightened geopolitical tensions. Hence, the role of the G20 has become even more critical today.

Rising protectionism is threatening the multilateral trading system. Protectionism, trade wars, sluggish economic growth all make it incumbent for G20 to deliberate on ways in which free trade flows can be promoted. This is necessary since hundreds of millions of people are yet to be fully integrated with the world economy and reap its full benefits. The global trading system will have to become fair and equitable. WTO needs to be further reformed to keep pace with the ever-changing and ever more complex global economy.

Friends, in a global economy, our actions and those of others are likely to have a global impact. Even if we are careful and considerate when it comes to technology, we still might be adversely impacting some other country and society located far away from us. That is the reality of today's world. At the same time, if growth is not fast enough and sustained over a long period of time, we would not be able to adequately deal with poverty. These are the kinds of challenges which forums such as this will have to deliberate on.

Global multilateral institutions, including global financial institutions, need further reforms to reflect the realities of the day. Reformed multilateralism is the need of the hour for these institutions to remain relevant. As the issue of IMF Quota and Governance Reforms and other proposals to give more voice and representation to Emerging and Developing Market Countries in IMF is being deliberated, the G20 has an important role in breaking the deadlock in the current negotiations.

Economies with liquidity should invest in economies where there is potential for expansion in order to sustain global growth. G20 should play a lead role in this regard. One of the key challenges faced by developing economies is the absence of coordinated policy measures from developed countries, resulting in reversal of funds from developing economies to developed economies.

India values its partnership with Japan; we look forward to working closely with Japan for the success of the Japanese Presidency and the 14th G20 Summit being held in June, at Osaka. India has always looked forward to working closely with G20 presidencies to forge consensus on various issues and we would do so during the Japanese Presidency as well. Our best wishes go out to Japan for its presidency.

We also think that the themes and focus areas identified by the Japanese Presidency are greatly relevant in today's world. Lack of infrastructure is a major impediment to realising socio-economic growth, especially of the developing countries. Therefore, we welcome the thrust on high-quality infrastructure. India has declared infrastructure as an asset class to enable larger investments into this sector. India believes that the G20 should also play a more active role in promoting infrastructure investments by multilateral development banks.

We welcome the focus being brought on ageing and the need to provide quality life to the aged as well. It is increasingly becoming an important area requiring greater attention in many countries. Indeed, this is an area which could benefit from the technological revolution.

Another critical agenda that would need to be taken forward during the 2019 presidency is the issue of skill deficiency, especially in developing economies. Interestingly, this is an area of concern even in developed economies with rapid technological changes. This was suitably reflected in the priorities of the Argentinian Presidency as "Future of Work."

Here, I would like to compliment Argentina for having organised the first ever joint meeting of the education and labour ministers, recognising the need for policy coordination to be initiated from the early days of schooling so that the transformation from schooling to employment is a smooth one. We urge Japan to continue to give focus to this area as it has emerged as a critical area of concern, exacerbating social tensions and resulting in restrictive policy measures.

G20 Leaders in Buenos Aires had agreed that WTO has played an important role in promoting a free, open, rules-based world trading order and had also agreed that there is a need for reforms in the WTO. We look forward to further discussions towards protecting and strengthening multilateral trading systems and reforming the WTO while retaining its core approach of differential treatment for developing economies amongst others.

Friends, PM Modi had highlighted at the Buenos Aires Summit the need to strengthen cooperation on returning economic fugitives and their illegally acquired assets. PM Modi has also stressed the need for G20 to work on strengthening social security schemes and ensure their portability. We look forward to further progress in this regard.

We also look forward to working closely to realise the shared objective of ensuring price stability in energy markets because this is impacting both the developed and the developing markets, the latter more so.

We look forward also to working closely with Japan during its presidency for taking forward the agenda on climate change, including implementation of commitment by developed countries to support the adaptation and mitigation efforts in developing countries on countering terrorism and on global health.

In conclusion, I would like to mention that India is looking forward to itself hosting the G20 Presidency in 2022, the 75th year of our independence. While we would build on the good work done by the previous presidencies, the government of India is also looking to create more opportunities and give a new thrust to global development and the community feeling, and in this regard, we look forward to receiving valuable inputs from the T20.

2019

Suresh Prabhu,

19 July, 2019[6]

Suresh Prabhu, G7 and G20 Sherpa for India and four-time Member of Parliament, spoke about India's growing prominence in the G20 and gave a summary of the Osaka Summit, at Gateway House

The reemergence of India over the past few years has happened as a process, and not overnight. Today, India is recognised as one of the important players in the world in almost all spheres of activity. In terms of the economy, of Purchasing Power Parity (PPP), India is third in the world, among the top economies. In dollar terms also (its GDP ranking) is sixth in the world. India's economy is strong at over $1.8 trillion, but the challenge is to realise that this amount is shared by around 1.3 billion people. The world may see the huge grand total. But per capita income is a domestic issue: we need to make sure that whatever wealth is generated is distributed and people have a good quality of life.

Another global issue is environment. As a part of the ministry of environment 20 years ago, I always said that India may not be a part of G7, but it is a part of P7 – "Potential Polluters 7." Environmental problems are the unfortunate outcome of economic activity, causing depletion of national resources (while producing this economic output). Therefore, they have an impact on us. When we become a large economy, people look at us as a market, and as a part of global supply chains, wherein we do not only sell products, but also source them…

Coming then to the G20, this is a grouping of countries whose economic output constitutes 85% of global GDP. The figures even within this are quite skewed as 20 economies out of the total number of countries – that is, about 10% – will have 85% of global output. It is an important forum. The G20 – unlike the G7, which comprises the world's seven largest economies – is a unique combination of the developed and developing nations. (Countries like Indonesia, Brazil, India and South Africa are economically in the first 20 but still cannot be called the most developed countries.) A decision taken by the G20 has far greater acceptability than that taken by any other forum that is more exclusive.

India has now become a key player in the G20, and I have followed G20's processes for a long time, having been India's Sherpa in 2014 too. G20 is maturing as a grouping, people know each other better from working together. The operational comfort between countries has increased. At the same time, because the G20 constitutes 85% of the global economy, if the global economy slows – and that is not in anybody's interest – every country will be affected.

The global economy has been slowing – despite some recovery after the 2008 crisis – and this can be attributed to trade. Global trade was the driving force of the global economy. Prior to 2008, commodities, which constituted the bulk of trade, were being taken across the globe in a very intensified manner, which led to trade and commodity growth being greater than the global economy's growth. Since the slowdown, countries are questioning the very basis of global trade. The governing body – the World Trade Organization – is raising existential issues. This is worrying. India strongly feels it must promote the WTO.

In 2017, following the collapse of talks at the Buenos Aires ministerial conference in December, we organised a "mini ministerial" meeting in New Delhi, which was attended by all 57 countries. And two months ago, we organised a similar event with only developing countries. We are planning to find out, in our own way, as Indians, how to ensure that global trade remains a robust and driving force in growth.

In the G20 declaration (at Osaka) issues related to both trade and economic growth were addressed, and I am glad that we played a key role in the formulation of the issues. For example, the other aspect of the economic issue is infrastructure growth. Infrastructure growth itself can spur economic activity. If the infrastructure of some countries is made to grow, this will induce demand from other countries since they will also benefit. An example of this is China's Belt and Road Initiative, which has aided its economic growth.

Some important social issues were also discussed at Osaka. Japan, as the President of the G20 summit, made a very welcome contribution, namely, Society 5.0, which covers how we can make a better society for the future by leveraging technology, how we can manage an aged society, and this is an area where India has a great role to play. We can train people in managing an ageing society. This is, after all, a global issue.

Women's empowerment was another area of discussion. In India, we encourage women-led growth: if all women became economically engaged that itself will help increase our country's GDP by 1%.

The discussions devoted much time to the environment, climate change, energy and the Paris Agreement, focus areas also for the G7. The oceans are, in a way, the last resort and hope for the environment, absorbing all that happens terrestrially. Marine biodiversity is far richer than terrestrial, biological diversity.

Climate change is not a topic for mere discussion at Gateway House, but a real-life issue for people. We must make sure that climate change becomes an integral part of foreign policy.

At the G20 Summit in Osaka, in June, Prime Minister Modi spoke of two other issues, namely, economic offenders, the main objective being to bring offenders back to the country where they committed the offence. Terrorism was the other. The panellists agreed that terrorism is a global issue, part of a global chain and the global community needs to plan actively on how to counter it.

Technology, another point of discussion, is an area where India has a major role to play. The digital world is around us. There are many conversations taking place about the Fourth Industrial Revolution, and the digital platform will be the foundation for it.

Each of these issues – be it technology or terrorism or ageing – global though they are, are important as they influence our day-to-day lives. We should be conscious of them and work on them.

Another facet emerging from all these developments is that people have started respecting India's opinion. Japan, for example, acknowledged India's contribution at the Osaka Summit. I am happy to inform that India is playing a constructive role and is moving forward. We have also been invited as a partner to the G7 Summit in France (24–26 August). Ambassador Suresh Reddy and I will be going ahead to prepare for the Prime Minister's visit. We share the responsibility of preparing for it, like we did at the G20 Summit in Osaka.

3.3 Direction provided by India's Prime Ministers at the G20[7]

Two Indian prime ministers have made an impact on the G20 – Dr. Manmohan Singh, whose speech in 2008 at the height of the financial crisis, called for the urgent reform of the existing multilateral financial systems, and Narendra Modi, who put India's agenda front and centre at the G20, and pursued it with determination.

Their statements at the G20 summits – Singh in 2008, and Modi from 2014–2020 – provide a clear understanding of India's direction in the global financial order.

Although this book deals with India in the G20 since 2015, it is instructive to reproduce Dr. Manmohan Singh's 2008 address at the G20, for that year was significant in making the G20 an expanded body that included both the developed and developing countries, making them equal partners in the global financial order.

15 November 2008:
Dr. Manmohan Singh, Summit of the Heads of State or Governments of the G-20 countries on Financial Markets and the World Economy, Washington, DC, USA.[8]

We are meeting at a time of exceptional difficulty for the world economy. The financial crisis, which a year ago seemed to be localised in one part of the financial system in the United States, has exploded into a systemic crisis, spreading through the highly interconnected financial markets of industrialised countries, and has had its effects on other markets also.

It has choked normal credit channels, triggered a worldwide collapse in stock markets around the world. The real economy is clearly affected. Industrialised countries were expected to slow down in 2008. They are now projected to be in a recession in the second half of the year, and there is as yet little prospect of an early recovery. Many have called it the most serious crisis since the Great Depression.

Emerging market countries were not the cause of this crisis, but they are amongst its worst affected victims. Recession will hit the export performance of developing countries and the choking of credit, combined with elevated risk perception, will lead to lower capital flows and reduced levels of foreign direct investment. The combined effect will be to slow down economic growth in developing countries.

India is experiencing this negative impact. After growing at close to 9% per year for four years, our growth rate is expected to slow down to between 7% and 7.5% in the current financial year. The pace of growth next year will depend, in part, upon how long the global recession lasts and how quickly global capital flows return to normal. Much of India's growth is internally driven and I expect we can maintain a strong pace of growth in the coming years, but many developing countries will be hit harder.

A slowing down of growth in developing countries will push millions of people back into poverty, with adverse effects on nutrition, health and education levels. These are not transient impacts but will impact a full generation. If we are to prevent a slide back and ensure that Millennium Development Goals are achieved, we need to ensure that growth in developing economies is not affected.

Since the crisis is global, it calls for a co-ordinated global response and this summit is, therefore, timely. In our discussions, we need to distinguish between the immediate priority, which must be to bring the crisis under control as quickly as possible with as little adverse effect on developing countries, and the medium-term objective of re-forming the global financial architecture to prevent similar crises in future. I will comment briefly on both.

As far as the immediate priority is concerned, I recognise that a number of important steps have already been taken by countries to inject liquidity into the financial system, recapitalise banks and other systemically important institutions. Some countries have also intro-duced a number of innovative, even unorthodox, measures to restore confidence so that the financial system could start functioning again. These measures have had some effect, but the crisis is far from over. Credit channels remain clogged and the signs of distress in the real economy suggest that additional measures are needed.

An obvious issue is to consider whether the emergence of recession-ary trends calls for some fiscal stimulus. A coordinated fiscal stimulus by countries that are in a position to do so would help mitigate the se-verity and duration of the recession. It would also send a strong signal to investors around the world. Resort to fiscal stimulus may be viewed as risky in some situations, but if we are, indeed, on the brink of the worst downturn since the Great Depression, the risk may be worth taking. We should, therefore, take all possible measures at the national level to complement any coordinated international stimulus.

The international community needs to consider special initiatives to counter the shrinkage of capital flows to developing countries that is almost certain to occur over the next two years.

The initiative by the IMF to establish a new liquidity facility is a welcome step. However, we must also consider whether the IMF is ad-equately funded for the task it will face in managing this global crisis. Looking ahead we must plan for possible additional demands on the IMF if the global recession is pronounced. This suggests that we must activate a process for replenishing IMF resources.

An alternative to the IMF as a source of quick disbursing liquidity is the establishment of short-term swap arrangements. The existence of such arrangements will reduce the burden on the IMF and will add to confidence in the system. Countries in a position to do so should consider the scope for expanding such arrangements.

Depressed conditions in the global economy are likely to produce a downturn in private investment in developing countries which will worsen recessionary trends. It is necessary to take steps to counter this development. Expanding investment in infrastructure by the pub-lic sector and also the private sector where possible is an ideal coun-tercyclical device. It has the immediate effect of stimulating demand countercyclically and the longer-term effect of laying the conditions for an early return to faster growth. Investment in infrastructure is today perhaps the best signal for reviving private investment, including FDI, tomorrow.

This requires new and innovative ways of solving the financing problems that will restrain infrastructure investment. The World Bank, regional development banks and national governments need to consider measures such as providing additional credit for infrastructure projects, promote new instruments for infrastructure financing and providing capital and liquidity support to banking institutions to lend to infrastructure projects that are underway.

The World Bank/IFC and the Regional Development banks should aim at making an additional $50 billion per year in support of infrastructure development in the public and private sectors. This window can be wound down once normalcy returns to global capital flows.

Industrialised countries can also help revive trade flows in developing countries by expanding the scale of export credit finance available to these countries. We know there is a temporary market failure in this area with elevated risk perceptions which discourage private flows. There is a need to intervene to overcome market failure. A collapse of trade is the last thing that one wants in the current crisis, with all its implications for growth and employment. Concerted government action in expanding export credit financing on reasonable terms will help support the pace of development in developing countries, which is critical for achieving poverty alleviation and employment objectives.

Our willingness to take specific steps to support developing countries in this period of exceptional difficulty will be a test of our collective leadership. Many developing countries have made strenuous efforts to implement economic reforms to deal with the challenges of an increasingly open and globalised world. This has often required the implementation of policies which have aroused domestic fears and uncertainties. We have persevered in this process and have benefited from it. Economic performance in almost all developing countries has improved. In the process, attitudes towards globalisation have begun to change and people all over the world have come to appreciate the enormous benefits that can be derived from global economic integration. It would be a great pity if this growing support for open policies in the developing world is weakened because of a failure to protect developing countries from a recession which is not of their making.

We need to take urgent steps to strengthen the global trading system and forestall any protectionist tendencies which always surface in times of recession. A successful conclusion of the ongoing multilateral trade talks would be an important confidence builder at this stage. We are willing to work constructively with other major players to reach a balanced and mutually beneficial outcome.

While our immediate priority should be to deal with the crisis which is still unfolding, we also need to look ahead to see what changes are needed in the global financial architecture to avoid such crisis from recurring. Much useful work in this area has already been done by Finance Ministers and there is considerable consensus on many areas. I will, therefore, limit my remarks to a few points.

I agree with the general consensus that there are several factors behind the crisis and the future global economic architecture must be designed to deal with these. These include failure of regulatory and supervisory mechanisms, inadequate appreciation and management of systemic risks and inadequate transparency in financial institutions.

The new architecture we design must include a credible system of multilateral surveillance, which can signal the emergence of imbalances that are likely to have systemic effects, and also put in motion a process of consultation that can yield results in terms of policy coordination. At this point, I would like to emphasise the importance of broad-based multilateral approaches to our efforts. Bodies such as the G-7 are no longer sufficient to meet the demands of the day. We need to ensure that any new architecture we design is genuinely multilateral with adequate representation from countries reflecting changes in economic realities.

The International Monetary Fund is the logical body to perform the task of multilateral surveillance of macro-economic imbalances and their relationship to financial stability. However, it is relevant to ask whether its systems and procedures are adequate to the task. Over the years, the Fund has become marginal to the task of policy analysis and consultations on macro-economic imbalances and related policies in the major countries. That task is now performed in other forums though it is questionable whether it is being performed well. I believe we need a comprehensive review of the procedures of the IMF, leading to recommendations on governance reform that would enable the Fund to perform the role of macro-economic policy coordination.

An important element of longer-term reform is to restructure the representation in the governance levels of the Fund to reflect the current and prospective economic realities. Quota reform is the normal way to effect a change in voting power, but it has been contentious and incremental, and what has been achieved thus far has fallen far short of what is needed. The Board of Governors of the IMF should be explicitly charged with exploring alternative modalities to achieve a more legitimate representation.

Looking ahead, we also have to pay attention to the many regulatory gaps in the financial system which allowed the development of excess leverage and the risks associated with it. It is obvious that we need better systems of risk management and better regulation and supervision, especially of institutions that have a global reach and are dealing in financial instruments that are exceedingly complex. Managers of financial institutions, credit rating agencies and regulators have to do a much better job. The structure of incentives in the system has to be aligned to this end. We also need to examine whether the existing forums of regulators that are there are adequate and cover the entire gamut of regulatory and supervisory activities that are required.

These are technical issues that should be tackled in the specialised forums dealing with financial stability, notably the Basle Committee on Banking Supervision and the Financial Stability Forum. However, both these bodies need to have broader representation than they do at present. International co-ordination on regulatory issues would be more easily achieved if the principal forums where these issues are discussed were seen to be more representative.

Broad basing the present representation in these forums is much easier to achieve and I hope this Summit will give a clear signal in this direction. It will certainly build confidence in our intention over the longer term to achieve significant reform in the governance of the global financial system.

Given the fact that this financial crisis has affected growth prospects across the board, we also need to examine the present structures of trade and development finance to consider how to ensure greater stability in these flows in the face of difficult situations such as the current one. This issue could be examined by the expert group I have referred to or by a separate group focusing on this issue. Its work could lead to the design of appropriate international mechanisms and instruments for maintaining and enhancing these flows in future.

The convening of this Summit has raised expectations in many circles that we will work to produce a new Bretton Woods II. The world has certainly changed sufficiently to need a new architecture, but this can only be done on the basis of much greater preparation and consultation. We can, however, signal that we are serious about starting a process that will, in time, produce an architecture suited to the new challenges and vulnerabilities facing the world economy and reflective of the changes that have taken place in the economic structure.

We must also give the world a clear signal of our resolve to take specific coordinated action to handle the current crisis in a manner, which restores confidence and which also responds to the needs of developing countries. We need to ensure that the processes we set in motion today safeguard and promote the welfare of our future generations.

2014–2020:
Since Prime Minister Modi's speeches are not available in public docu-
ments, the following are the links to the Official Summaries or Excerpts
from the Official Media Briefings of the G20 Summits by India's G20
Sherpas, and Official Statements given from 2014, 2015, 2016, 2017,
2018, 2019 through to 2020.

2014:
Prime Minister Narendra Modi at the G20 Leaders' Summit, Bris-
bane, Australia, his first G20 Leaders' Summit.
India Focus: Black Money and Illegal flow of funds
India's G20 Sherpa: Suresh Prabhu

**Transcript of Media Briefing on forthcoming G20 Summit (6 November
2014)**
    06 November 2014[9]

3.3.1 *Official Spokesperson:*

This is Prime Minister's first participation at the G20 Summit and Mr.
(Suresh) Prabhu is also participating as the Sherpa for the first time.
We have a continuity in terms of our sous-sherpas. On the extreme
right is Ms. Usha Titis, Joint Secretary in the Ministry of Finance and
she is the sous-sherpa for the financial track. On my left is Mr. Charan-
jeet Singh who is Joint Secretary (MER) in the Ministry of External
Affairs and who assists on other issues. May I now request Mr. Suresh
Prabhu to make his opening remarks.

3.3.2 *Shri Suresh Prabhu:*

The Brisbane G20 is continuation of many things that have happened
since 2008. But also in a way it is an important milestone. Firstly, as
you all know 2008 was a very critical year for the global economy. We
had a contraction, we had a virtual questioning of the entire economic
model that we have been working for a long time. We were believing
that the world economy is going to go in only one direction, it is going
to continuously expand and that was particularly questioned in this
2008 crisis. It started with financial institutions and then snowballed
into a virtual economic crisis which affected not just countries who
were responsible for it but also some other countries. Then there was
a realisation that dawned that there are not just 7–8 countries of the

world which till then were like a club and who could deal with such a massive crisis that is engulfing the world; therefore, large emerging economies who have substantially large stakes because they suffered because of the economic crisis, but they could also rescue the rest of the world in terms of bringing back the growth and that is how in 2008 there was the first one (G20).

For more, see link: https://www.mea.gov.in/media-briefings.htm?dtl/24202/Transcript+of+Media+Briefing+on+forthcoming+G20+Summit+November+6+2014

2015

Prime Minister Narendra Modi at G20 Leaders' Summit at Antalya, Turkey

16 November 2015[10]

India focus: Climate Change, lowered cost of remittances

3.3.3 *Official Spokesperson:*

Friends, it is a great privilege for us to have with us Dr. Arvind Panagariya, who is Vice Chairman of NITI Aayog and the Sherpa for the G-20. As I mentioned to you, very hectic negotiations are still going on, on the final communiqué of the G-20…We also have with us Mrs. Usha Titus, who is Joint Secretary in the Department of Economic Affairs and is also one of the key Indian negotiators on the G-20.

3.3.4 *Sherpa G-20: (Dr. Arvind Panagaria):*

So, finally, we are here I think fourth or fifth day for me in Antalya. Truly very tough and rough days. We have had very very intense negotiations as you could judge from the activity that was going on still. So, perhaps as of now the negotiations are still not completely over. We negotiated day before yesterday till about 1:30 at night. Yesterday outstanding issues remained and we went back to negotiating table around 10:30 or 11 and then we are negotiating till 4 o'clock. When we left we thought that the negotiation was hopefully over by then, but I think there are still some small outstanding issues remaining. In any case, I think till the communiqué itself is released, I cannot tell you what is in the communiqué or what will be in the communiqué because we are still waiting for the final word on it.

For more, see link: https://www.mea.gov.in/interviews.htm?dtl/26042/Transcript+of+Media+Briefing+by+Official+Spokesperson+and+Sherpa+G20+in+Antalya+November+16+2015

2016
PM Modi at the G20 Leaders' Summit, Huangzhou, China
4–5 September 2016[11]
Prime Minister led the Indian delegation to the 11th G20 Summit in
Hangzhou, China, on 4–5 September 2016. The leaders discussed the issues of policy coordination and breaking new path for growth, more effective and efficient global economic and 12 financial governance, robust
international trade and investment, inclusive and interconnected development and other issues affecting world economy. The G20 Leaders issued a Communiqué at the Summit. An Informal Meeting of BRICS
Leaders was held on 4 September 2016 on the margins of the G20 Summit in Hangzhou, China. The meeting was chaired by Prime Minister.
    The Leaders held wide-ranging discussions on the G20 Summit
Agenda and agreed to pursue issues of global and mutual interest to
the BRICS countries at the G20. Besides, the leaders exchanged views
on a wide range of global political, security, economic and global governance issues of importance and mutual concern. The Leaders reit-
erated their wholehearted commitment to the fight against terrorism
in all its forms and manifestations, with the United Nations playing a
central role.

2017 July 7, 2017, G20 Leaders' Summit, Hamburg, Germany
11-Point agenda on Counter Terrorism
Transcript of Media Briefing in Hamburg on G20 Summit (08 July 2017)
08 July 2017[12]

3.3.5 *Official Spokesperson, Shri Gopal Baglay:*

I have with me the Vice Chairman of NITI Aayog and Sherpa for G20,
Dr. Arvind Panagariya. Next to him is Dr. Tapan Ray, Secretary, Department of Economic Affairs who deals with the finance track, the
Finance Deputy Shri Sameer Khare, who is Joint Secretary in the Ministry of Finance dealing with multilateral relations, and my good friend
Alok Dimri, who is the Director General or Joint Secretary in the Ministry of External Affairs dealing with multilateral economic relations.

3.3.6 *Vice Chairman NITI Aayog, Dr. Arvind Panagariya:*

Thank you Gopal. Let me just say first, thank you for being here. We
negotiated, over the past few days, I'll describe you the process also, the
G20 Communique. My colleagues here were all very actively involved,
Secretary DEA negotiated the finance track and then I assisted Mr.
Khare and Mr. Alok Dimri negotiated the rest of the communique.

The process this time was even longer drawn, this was my third summit communique negotiation and this by far the longest negotiation. I arrived on the morning of 4th July from Delhi and we got started at around 1 pm and since then we probably have been sleeping about four hours or so every night. So you can count the hours from 4 to 7 July, i.e. four days and taking out the around 20 hours of sleep so we have been negotiating for pretty much 76 hours.

This is very long drawn and this was partially so because it was not totally unpredictable given the changes that have happened in the governments around the world especially the United States but also the United Kingdom where the view of governments have shifted from where it had been traditionally so that also meant that at least in some particular areas the negotiation was difficult and that accounts for a very large extent for the time it took. That's not the only thing, it's also the individual personalities involved in the negotiations and sometimes there is a lot of discussion on some specific phrasing, re-phrasing, inclusion, not-inclusion, etc., that's the process.

For more, see link: https://mea.gov.in/media-briefings.htm?dtl/28731/ Media+Briefing+in+Hamburg+on+G20+Summit+Uncorrected+ translation+July+08+2017

2018
30 November 2018, G20 Leaders' Summit, Buenos Aires, Argentina[13]
In 2018, Prime Minister Modi placed India's concerns on Fugitive Economic offences on the G20 Agenda. He made nine points:

- Strong and active cooperation across G-20 countries to deal comprehensively and efficiently with the menace fugitive economic offenders.
- Cooperation in the legal processes such as effective freezing of the proceeds of crime; early return of the offenders and efficient repatriation of the proceeds of crime should be enhanced and streamlined.
- Joint effort by G-20 countries to form a mechanism that denies entry and safe havens to all fugitive economic offenders.
- Principles of United Nations Convention Against Corruption (UNCAC), United Nations Convention Against Transnational Organized Crime (UNOTC), especially related to "International Cooperation" should be fully and effectively implemented.
- Financial Action Task Force (FATF) should be called upon to assign priority and focus to establishing international co-operation that leads to timely and comprehensive exchange of information between the competent authorities and FIUs.

- FATF should be tasked to formulate a standard definition of fugitive economic offenders.
- FATF should also develop a set of commonly agreed and standardised procedures related to identification, extradition and judicial proceedings for dealing with fugitive economic offenders to provide guidance and assistance to G-20 countries, subject to their domestic law.
- Common platform should be set up for sharing experiences and best practices including successful cases of extradition, gaps in existing systems of extradition and legal assistance.
- G-20 Forum should consider initiating work on locating properties of economic offenders who have a tax debt in the country of their residence for its recovery.

2019
PM Modi at G20 Leaders' Summit at Osaka, Japan
21 June 2019
Media Briefing by G20 Sherpa on visit of Prime Minister to Japan to attend G20 Summit (21 June 2019)[14]
24 June 2019

3.3.7 *Official Spokesperson, Shri Raveesh Kumar*

Welcome to this special briefing on Prime Minister's visit to Osaka, Japan, for the 14th G20 Summit from 27 to 29 June. For our Prime Minister Shri Narendra Modi, this will be the sixth time that he will be participating at the G20 Summit… On the dais Prime Minister's Sherpa for the G20 Summit Shri Suresh Prabhu. I also have Joint Secretary (MER) in the Ministry of External Affairs, Shri Suresh Reddy.

3.3.8 *G20 Sherpa, Shri Suresh Prabhu*

Good afternoon friends. As you know over a period of time and particularly after the peak economic shock of 2008, the G20 has become a very important global platform for dealing with, to begin with, economic issues and now over a period of time many other important global issues. And G20 being obviously consisting of such members who together contribute to almost 85% of global GDP, economic issues assume great importance and particularly in the light of so many interesting developments recently, in the light of the year about global slowdown, I am sure one of the very important issues that will be discussed in the G20 Summit in Osaka later next week will be the economic issue.

Other issues also get discussed and one of them inevitably is linked to energy and environment; they are the two sides of the same coin. What kind of energy we are going to use and India will be able to showcase its great remarkable strides into changing the energy mix which, in turn, can also result into global change of energy mix.

For more, read link: https://mea.gov.in/media-briefings.htm?dtl/31463/Transcript+of+Media+Briefing+by+G20+Sherpa+on+visit+of+Prime+Minister+to+Japan+to+attend+G20+Summit+June+21+2019

2020
15th G20 Leaders' Summit
21 November 2020, New Delhi

1 Prime Minister, Shri Narendra Modi, participated in the 15th G20 Summit convened by Saudi Arabia, on 21–22 November 2020. The Summit, which saw participation of respective Heads of State/Government of 19 member countries, EU, other invited countries and international organisations, was conducted in virtual format in view of the COVID-19 pandemic.

2 PM congratulated the Kingdom of Saudi Arabia and its leadership for its successful Presidency of the G20 this year and for organising the second G20 Summit in 2020 through a virtual format despite the challenges and obstacles posed by the COVID-19 pandemic.

3 The Summit under Saudi Presidency centred on the theme "Realising Opportunities of 21st Century for All" which has assumed greater importance in the wake of the ongoing COVID-19 pandemic. The agenda of the Summit is spread out over two days with two sessions focused on overcoming the pandemic, economic recovery and restoring jobs, and building an inclusive, sustainable and resilient future. There are also side events planned on the two days on pandemic preparedness and on safeguarding the planet.

4 PM termed the COVID-19 pandemic as an important turning point in history of humanity and the biggest challenge the world is facing since the World War II. He called for decisive action by G20, not limited to economic recovery, jobs and trade, but to focus on preserving Planet Earth noting that all of us are trustees of humanity's future.

5 PM called for a new Global Index for the Post-Corona World that comprises four key elements – creation of a vast Talent Pool; ensuring that Technology reaches all segments of the society; Transparency in systems of governance and dealing with Mother Earth with a spirit of Trusteeship. Based on this, the G20 can lay the foundation of a new world.

6 PM underscored that in the past few decades, while there has been an emphasis on Capital and Finance, the time has come to focus on Multi-Skilling and Re-skilling to create a vast Human Talent Pool. This would not only enhance dignity of citizens but also make our citizens more resilient to face crises. He also said that any assessment of new technology should be based on its impact on Ease of Living and Quality of Life.

7 He called for greater Transparency in governance systems which will inspire our citizens to deal with shared challenges and enhance their confidence. He also said that dealing with environment and nature as trustees rather than owners will inspire us towards a Holistic and Healthy Life Style, a principle whose benchmark could be a Per Capita Carbon Footprint.

8 Noting that "Work from Anywhere" is a new normal in the post-COVID world, PM also suggested creation of a G20 Virtual Secretariat as a follow-up and documentation repository.

9 The 15th G20 Leaders' Summit would continue on 22 November 2020 culminating in the adoption of the Leaders' Declaration and with Saudi Arabia passing on the Presidency to Italy.

3.4 Turkey and Argentina present their views

2015: Turkey, G20 President.

Excerpts from the Remarks at the T20 meeting, Mumbai, by Dr. Burak Akçapar, Ambassador of Turkey to India, 19 October 2015.[15]

The Road to Antalya and Istanbul Summits
Transformation of the Global Development and Humanitarian Agenda

It is, indeed, an honour to address the Mumbai meeting of the Think 20. The forum serves as an ideas bank and offers an essential input to the debates on policy issues taken up by the G20. As such it is a challenge to address such august audience whose lives are devoted to thinking. I thank TEPAV and the Gateway House for organising this important meeting.

Turkey and India, as two emerging stars, have been putting their collective energy into taking their relations to new levels. Both bilaterally and globally, this is an era in which our thinking caps are again much needed. The world is undergoing a transformation. Such periods need transformative agendas.

2015 and 2016 have emerged as transformative years for the global agenda to leave no one behind in terms of the three interdependent main pillars of the United Nations, namely peace and security and development and human rights which celebrates its 70th anniversary.

In September 2015, the Millennium Development Goals were replaced by the Sustainable Development Goals and the Agenda 2030.

The Agenda 2030, Addis Ababa Action Agenda and the Paris Conference document on climate change will establish the framework of the global development agenda for the next 15 years. In between the 12th session of the Conference of the Parties to the United Nations Convention to Combat Desertification (UNCCD) is being held on 12–23 October 2015 in Ankara.

This will be followed by the G20 Summit in Antalya which is the culmination point of the Turkish Presidency of the G20 and some 100 meetings that were organised in this context.

The 10th WTO Ministerial Conference will be held in Nairobi, Kenya, from the 15 to 18 December 2015. A positive outcome in this Conference will shape the global trade and investment framework in the post-2015 development agenda. It will provide the necessary impetus to enhance trade and investment.

The transformation of the global agenda will be complete on 23–24 May 2016 with the first ever World Humanitarian Summit to be held in Istanbul. This Summit will bring together governments, humanitarian organisations, people affected by humanitarian crises and new partners including the private sector to propose solutions to our most pressing challenges and set an agenda to keep humanitarian action fit for the future. Particular focus will be on the G20 group of nations, individually or collectively, in helping fund facilitate this transformation.

When G20 Leaders met first time in 2008, they set their main objective as "achieving strong, sustainable and balanced growth"... They also noted that G20 plays key role in achieving this objective as the "premier platform for international economic cooperation."

In the seven years since the onset of the global financial crisis, global growth continues to be moderate. It has been around 3–3.5% range over the past five years.

Global growth is also uneven. In advanced economies, it is on average around 2.5% while it differs significantly from country to country.

In emerging economies, growth has been decelerating from around 6% to 4.5–5%...While the low-income developing countries continue to demonstrate a strong growth performance, as they integrate more to the global economy, they have become more open to the risks caused by developments in global economy.

As the G20 Presidency, Turkey added "inclusive growth" to the G20 goal of achieving strong, sustainable and balanced growth.

But this process needs better coordination.

Turkey has highlighted three I's. These have been implementation, investment and inclusiveness. On implementation, our aim is to ensure that G20 walks the talk. Confidence is the best and most effective way of attracting investments and sustaining economic growth. If fully implemented, the G20 growth strategies adopted last year will lift the G20's GDP by 2.1% by 2018.

This means more than 2 trillion US Dollars would be added to the global economy, which will create millions of jobs and raise non-G20 GDP by over 0.5%. This additional growth is much needed given that global growth continues to fall short of expectations. This year we developed a robust framework to hold ourselves accountable for our growth strategies, including detailed implementation schedules.

On investment, our priority is to take action for closing the global infrastructure gap. It is estimated that 70 trillion Dollars of investment is needed for the next 15 years.

In Addis Ababa Action Agenda, it is highlighted that developing countries need around 1.5 trillion Dollars of investment annually to pursue their sustainable development efforts. Therefore, investment is crucial for developed and developing countries alike.

In this context, we have prepared country-specific investment strategies to improve the investment ecosystem, foster efficient infrastructure investment and support financing opportunities for SMEs. This will help us to monitor progress and see how the G20 can coordinate efforts in increasing infrastructure investments at the global scale.

The third "I," namely inclusiveness, aims to ensure the benefits of growth and prosperity are shared by people within and beyond G20 countries.

Women and youth deserve particular attention since they constitute major vulnerable groups need to have a better share from prosperity and economic growth. Last year, the G20 made a commitment to reduce the **gender gap** in labour force participation by 25% until 2025. Effective implementation of this target will bring an additional 100 million women into the workforce.

Under the Turkish Presidency, a Women-20 was established as a standalone engagement group to promote gender inclusive economic growth and take steps to ensure women's effective participation into the economic life.

This year, Turkish Presidency focused also on reducing **youth unemployment**. G20 Labour Ministers adopted a G20 target on reducing the share of young people who are at most risk of being permanently left behind in the labour market by 15% by 2025.

Small and Medium Size Enterprises (SMEs) are another important element of our inclusiveness agenda. SMEs are the major source of employment and an important driver of economic growth in many countries. Turkish Presidency has decided to establish for the first time a World SME Forum in cooperation with the International Chamber of Commerce.

Encouraging the growth of SMEs is a sub-goal under the Sustainable Development Goal 8 on inclusive and sustainable economic growth. Therefore, G20's focus on SMEs is highly related to the Agenda 2030.

The inclusive growth agenda also contains an external dimension… Our aim here is to ensure that our decisions and actions will benefit not only G20 countries but also the entire world economy, including low-income developing countries…In this direction, Turkish G20 Presidency organised the first-ever joint meeting of G20 Finance Ministers and Finance Ministers from low-income developing countries.

In fact, G20 has its own development agenda coming from 2010 with several concrete and action-oriented elements. Five priority areas agreed by G20 members under the development agenda are infrastructure, domestic resources mobilisation, financial inclusion and remittances, food security and nutrition and human resources development. G20 development agenda is linked with several SDGs.

For instance, G20's work on food security is closely connected to SDG 2 on ending hunger, achieving food security and improved nutrition and promote sustainable agriculture and SDG 12 on ensuring sustainable consumption and production patterns. This year, we organised G20 Agriculture Ministers meeting in May.

Our focus is on regulatory and policy frameworks, access to financing and technology. This year, Turkey organised the first-ever G20 Energy Ministers meeting on 2 October 2015. Energy Ministers adopted the G20 Access to Energy Action Plan with a particular focus on Sub-Saharan Africa.

The private sector's role in development is very important if we are to succeed in developing more opportunities. Access to trade and technology facilitation are key components of SDG 17. This year we have focused on how firms in low-income developing countries, in particular SMEs, can participate in Global Value Chains.

We will also deliver a G20 Leaders' Call on Inclusive Business to promote opportunities for low-income people and communities to participate in markets. One of the key messages is to CEOs and companies. Inclusive business can be good business.

We all acknowledge that development is not just about assisting developing countries. Official Development Assistance (ODA) continues to be the most important source to support the development efforts of many countries, particularly the LDCs. UN members should meet their ODA commitments in full and a timely manner. As a matter of fact, ODA of Turkey was 1 billion dollars in 2010. In 2014, it was 3.5 billion dollars.

The emergence of non-traditional contributors, in addition to the established ones represented at the Developing Assistance Committee of the OECD, furnishes additional opportunities to sustain global humanitarian and development action.

Turkey is one such emerging donor whose contributions, now surpassing several of the established players, have qualified her to rank among the leading providers of ODA globally. A distinguishing characteristic of Turkey, in this regard, has been the dexterity with which she has positioned herself as a connector between East-West and North-South.

As an ODA receiving higher middle-income country, Turkey has achieved highest percentages of increase in her international development assistance including humanitarian assistance funding in a diversity of regions. She has shouldered the heaviest burden in terms of the number of displaced persons escaping Syrian and DAESH brutality.

The Syrian crisis shows that the humanitarian system requires urgent repair. This requires a new look at structures, financing and capacities. However, this would not be enough. The task is to expand the humanitarian space and humanise the overall system. The world needs a new humanitarian vision.

The Istanbul Summit will aim to build on the momentum of the SDGs in order to strengthen the capacity of the countries and communities as well as the international agencies to better cope with crises and natural and manmade disasters.

The World Humanitarian Summit is an opportunity to unify the global agendas for development behind a robust, effective and fresh vision of humanitarianism that would be the product for the first time in history of both the east and the west and the north and the south.

2018
Excerpts from an Interview with Pedro Villagra Delgado, G20 Sherpa, Argentina[16]

[In Argentina], we took into account the legacy of all the previous G20 presidencies because the show didn't start with us. We have been working with the G20 since its inception in 1999, and after it became a summit-level exercise in 2008. So, of course, we have to continue all the work that has been done in the previous presidencies.

Argentina's priorities at the G20 will be first, the future of work, including education, to give people the skills necessary for the changes taking place in the labour market and (to prepare for) digitalisation. The three go together. You just listened to the Minister of

Entrepreneurship and Information Technology of Estonia, Urve Palo, speak about the importance of digitalisation in that country's economy. That is true everywhere. The other priorities are investment in infrastructure for development and the future of food security.

Food security is not just about the provision of abundant, healthy and nutritious food but also the inclusion of food production in the global value chain. I think these are the three major priorities, with a perspective on gender to be included in every single item of the agenda, including the finance track and one on anti-corruption as well.

Of course, we have other things as well that we are going to have to tackle during the Argentine Presidency as previous presidencies have. These include climate change, the question of trade in services, financial flows and the importance of regulation in financial markets. We have to keep these in mind since the core business of the G20 is stability and governance of finance and micro-economics.

I think there is room for collaboration between India, Argentina, all other developing countries and the developed members of the G20 in all the areas that I mentioned. We have to close the inequality gap that is increasing around the world, not just in the developing countries, but also in the developed ones.

An important aspect of this is that we have to make sure that the Sustainable Development Goals – the 2030 agenda for development – are also implemented, that we get financing and have everybody come together to make sure people live decent lives and have good jobs in the future because that is also going to contribute to stability and governance, not just in the financial and macroeconomic sectors, but more broadly as well.

We all have to work together. That's what I'm here for.

One of the first things I did since taking up the presidency of the G20 was to start maintaining contact with the developing countries within the G20. I have contact with the Latin American countries obviously, as you can imagine. But I have gone to Africa because it is important not just for the members of the G20 to listen to them but also for the non-members to know things that are relevant to them since whatever the G20 decides, or comes to a consensus on regarding implementation, will probably affect the countries that are not sitting around the table. So I think it is only fair to have outreach to them.

Then, I went to Saudi Arabia, Indonesia and, now, India. We want to have the vision from the South, as Argentine President Macri has said. We have to have a G20 that is people-centred also, taking into account poverty reduction – and its elimination if possible. India's help in this and cooperation between Argentina and India is going to be very important, for us. And with all the contacts that I have made here during my visit to Delhi and Mumbai, I think we are both on the right track.

3.5 T20 commentary from Gateway House, at Gateway House[17]

Ussal Sahbaz, CEO, Centre for Economics and Foreign Policy Studies (EDAM), Istanbul; Manager, B20 and T20 Engagement Groups, Turkey as G20 President, 2015.
24 January 2019

3.5.1 Designing a global framework for fintech

Finance constitutes the core of the G20, which started as a finance ministers' meeting in 1997. Innovation and the digital economy are relatively new themes at the G20. The first innovation theme was adopted by the Think 20 Turkey in 2015; innovation became a priority of the Chinese G20 Presidency in 2016, and Germany brought the digital economy ministers together for the first time in 2017. Now, it is time to bring these old and new themes together and turn the G20 into a premier policy discussion forum around fintech, which refers to technology-enabled innovation that transforms financial services.

A G20 discussion around fintech is needed because of the emergence of global technology giants as data intermediaries, expanding into the financial services industry, resulting in regulatory risks and challenges. The panel on fintech at the official Think20 Mumbai Roundtable, organised by Gateway House on 28 January 2019, could not be more timely.

There are two dimensions to technology in finance: fintech and Techfin. While the abovementioned definition of fintech refers to fintech *as an activity*, fintech *as an entity* means "a non-bank institution that uses advanced technologies to perform traditional banking activities." These are usually startups, begun around consumer pain points in the financial services industry. Techfin refers to a company that starts with collecting consumer data for resolving a consumer pain point in a non-financial area and then utilising the same data to move into financial services.

Fintechs are financial intermediaries, whereas Techfins are data intermediaries. Techfins include American big-tech companies, such as Apple, Amazon, Microsoft, Google, Facebook, and new unicorns like Uber as well as Chinese big-tech, such as Alibaba, Tencent and

Baidu. Ant Financial, the financial services arm of Alibaba, reached a valuation of $150 billion – on a par with Unilever or Pepsi – in 2018 by building its services on the e-commerce data of its parent company. That said, the backbone of the global financial system is still the regular bank. An important principle under which banks operate is "territoriality." Although many banks have cross-border investments, each of the national units is regulated locally. Banks are the major tools through which monetary and macroprudential policymaking is conducted.

In contrast, Techfins generally act as if "they are on par with, not subordinate to, the countries that try to regulate them" and in a sense provide a global neutral environment to their users. They are sometimes called "Digital Switzerland." The power of Techfins stems from the trust they create in other consumer industries on which they collect vast amounts of consumer data. Amazon, for example, is the second most trusted institution in the United States, after the military.

In contrast, popular trust in the banking system is so low that in June 2018, Switzerland's electorate voted on a referendum calling for the country's commercial banks to be banned from creating money. Although the outcome was negative, even the fact that the central pillar of modern macroeconomic policy was being questioned by the electorate in one of the most important banking hubs of the world is telling. Techfins can increasingly make it harder to conduct financial policymaking and increase the financial risks, especially for the countries they are born in.

Fintechs, instead of building business models based on existing data repositories, generally start with customer pain points in a nation. Instead of transferring trust from another industry's customer relations, fintechs build trust by solving customer problems – usually creating totally new markets that have not been served by the banks so far and creating platforms for other entrepreneurs to tap and grow.

This is true in emerging markets inasmuch as, and probably even more than, in advanced markets. One example, iyzico, is a payment services company in Turkey. By offering payment services to entrepreneurs who cannot get access to traditional solutions offered by the banks, iyzico created a success story in financial inclusion. Small- and medium-sized businesses that use iyzico, on average, have grown 77% in size since 2016. The exports over iyzico have grown nine times larger than Turkey's average e-exports and reach on average a distance of 60% away from its home base.

Fintechs provide a wide range of services to customers that traditionally a bank undertakes – usually in a more innovative and customer-centric fashion and by making better use of technology-enabled innovation. This is sometimes called "unbundling of a bank" as illustrated in the figure above. This is why banks generally perceive fintechs as competitors.

Nevertheless, banks have some of the most traditional institutional structures, putting procedures ahead of consumer pain points, and data and ideas inside silos of different departments. It is unlikely that they can win the race of financial innovation with the Techfins. One way for the banks to stay ahead of the curve is, instead of approaching fintechs as competitors, to explore ways of cooperating with them to foster innovation. Such a strategy would be a win for fintechs as well, by providing them access to customer scale, brand reputation and domain expertise. Some banks are already pioneers in collaborating with fintechs. For instance, Bank Santander, which is based in Spain with a significant amount of operations in emerging markets, invests in fintech companies, including Ripple, a blockchain-based global financial settlement platform, and Kabbage, a leading automated credit provider to SMEs.

Regulatory change and guidance is key to incentivising (and sometimes forcing) banks to cooperate with the fintechs. Without proper regulatory incentives, banks are likely to act with short-term incentives to keep their balance sheets profitable, until the Techfins step in. It is worth noting that Google got an EU-wide e-money and payment services license in January 2019. Given the need for a balanced approach for the role of Techfins, for banks and fintechs to ensure functional financial policymaking, and for better financial inclusion and improved consumer welfare, the G20 can do the following:

- *Discuss optimal regulatory principles that will enable banks and fintechs to work together.* The new version of the Payment Services Directive in the EU (PSD2) is a case in point. It obliges banks to provide open access to their data, use transparent pricing schemes and avoid price discrimination in the infrastructure services they provide.
- *Discuss optimal structures to improve mutual learning for fintech regulatory sandboxes.* It is usually not possible to experiment with new fintech products under the regulations established for the traditional banks. Without the learning from experimentation, innovation becomes limited. Regulatory sandboxes, which now exist in more than 20 jurisdictions around the world, enable fintechs to conduct certain transactions and services within defined

threshold limits, while full compliance is ensured once the testing is completed and the business becomes more established.

• *Establish a forum to identify best practices around government-led infrastructure investments for the development of fintechs.* One such infrastructure is digital identification, which enables electronic know-your-customer applications or payment applications through ID cards.

For example, India's Aadhaar system provided digital identification to 1.2 billion people. The privacy and ethical issues should also constitute a part of the G20 discussion around government-led interventions. Another relevant infrastructure is Legal Entity Identifier (LEI), a unique global code for legal entities to increase financial stability by tracking the beneficial ownership of companies, mandated by the G20 Cannes Summit of 2011. The privacy and ethical issues should also constitute a part of the G20 discussion around government-led interventions.

3.5.2 LEI, a gold standard for financial transparency[18]

14 September 2018

Purvaja Modak, former Researcher, Geoeconomics Studies Programme, Gateway House

The 2008 global financial crisis, increasing instances of money laundering, terrorist financing and tax evasion revealed the lack of transparency in cross-border financial transactions. The Lehman Brothers' crisis, in particular, highlighted the importance of identifying the ownership structures of legal entities engaged in such transactions to better understand the systemic risks arising out of these linkages. In response, the G20 countries called for greater transparency in cross-border financial transactions.

At the G20 Cannes Summit of 2011, the G20-supported FSB was mandated by the G20 leaders with the task of delivering recommendations on the creation and implementation of a unique global code, called the LEI. In 2014, the LEI came into legal effect.

What exactly is the LEI? The LEI contains within it, two parts of an entity's lineage: who is who and who owns whom. This, a 20-digit alphanumeric code, holds standardised reference information on legal entities that participate in global financial transactions, serving as a proof of identity. This is basic business card information, giving clarity on "who is who" among market participants.

Its database, the Global LEI Index, is gradually being developed to identify an entity's direct and ultimate parents, answering the question of "who owns whom." The Global Legal Entity Identifier Foundation (GLEIF) leads the implementation process. It designates local operating units (LOUs) around the world, which provide registration and renewal facilities.

An entity can register[19] with any LOU of its choice, provided it lies in the LOU's jurisdiction. Typically, these LOUs are part of a country's official financial system. In India, for instance, the LEI is issued by the Legal Entity Identifier India Ltd. (LEIL), a wholly-owned subsidiary of the Clearing Corporation of India, and is governed by the Reserve Bank of India. In the United States, the sponsoring authority is the U.S. Commodity Futures Trading Commission – but private financial services player, Bloomberg, is also authorised to issue LEIs. In China, it is the China Financial Standardisation Technical Committee.

The information disclosed by the registrant is stored by the LOU in its database. It is publicly available and free of charge. It is reviewed, updated and validated by the LEI holder and the LOU through an annual renewal process. Banks, credit rating agencies and other institutions can access this database to gather accurate and credible information on their clients. LEIs, in addition, can help process letters of credit quicker and help identify sellers and suppliers on e-invoicing networks worldwide.

It can reduce business losses caused when transactions are rejected due to inadequate information or delays while on-boarding clients. A 2017 McKinsey study estimates that the use of LEIs in capital markets will reduce operational costs for the global investment banking industry by 3.5%, generating annual savings worth over $150 million.

LEI has plenty of takers. At the moment, capital markets participants who trade in over-the-counter (OTC) derivatives have been early adopters of the LEI; Canada, the EU, India, Mexico, Russia, Singapore, Switzerland and the United States were the first to accept it. Gradually, all entities, engaged in a wide range of cross-border transactions, will have to obtain an LEI.

To enable this, the administrative capacity and infrastructure of issuing LOUs must be improved.

Each country has its own official LEI issuer, and a unique response to participate in the LEI. India's issuer is the LEIL. In 2017, the Reserve Bank of India (RBI) set phased deadlines for legal entities to obtain LEIs, failing which they would not be eligible to participate in OTC derivative markets. Companies were slow to respond and missed the deadline of 31 March 2018. But now there is a rush to apply, and the deadline has been extended to 30 September 2018.

So far, 11,521[20] LEIs have been issued in India and as of 11 September 2018, 2,210 are pending acceptance. The slow pace of adoption – not just in India – is not surprising. LEI issuers and registrants have both reported that the process is complex and tiresome. Since the information is self-declared, the registrant is responsible for its accuracy. The issuers have reported that the registrants are oblivious of the requirements, and the declared information is incomplete and of poor quality. They also do not notify the issuer on new information, leading to inconsistencies, delays and data gaps – and potential loss of business for not being on board, on time.

This is a particular challenge for LOUs, which have to manually validate it, using official regulatory documents and private legal records.

However, the LEI is the gold standard of identifier information. A comparative study by Gateway House with other identification numbers used in India revealed that LEI's database is the only repository in the country that captures the relationship between the legal entity and its direct and ultimate parents. This gives India a strong rationale for extending the adoption of the LEI to any legal entity beyond those that trade in the OTC market.

The table below shows how superior the LEI's documentation is: it includes additional information like the shareholding structure, names and financial statements of the direct and ultimate parents. This database can be a one-stop destination for individuals, corporations, academics, media-seeking complete reference information on an entity and regulators and governments, who can get special access.

A salient feature of the LEI is that it can be integrated with other identification codes and processes. SWIFT's full BIC-to-LEI mapping initiative is a case in point. It is being explored by global software firms like R3, as the primary identifier that can integrate with solutions like distributed ledgers, connecting and cross-referencing all available information on an entity.

As of September 2018, 1,267,387 LEIs have been issued in 223 countries and 83,652 direct and ultimate parents have been identified. The largest number of registrations was reported in the United States, the United Kingdom, Germany, the Netherlands and Italy. Regulatory requirements in the Dodd-Frank Act of the United States and the European Union's Markets in Financial Instruments Directive and Regulation have made it compulsory for entities to adopt LEIs. Also, in the United States and the European Union, many issuers have been designated to issue LEIs, encouraging a larger number of registrations.

LEI applications in India, Estonia, Portugal, Mexico and Slovenia have gradually risen compared to previous quarters. The trend in India is attributed to the RBI's phased implementation deadlines.

Table 3.1 A comparison of identification numbers/codes in India

Number/Code	Purpose	Information Disclosed
Corporate Identification Number (CIN)	It is issued to every company incorporated in India when it is registered by the Registrar of Companies (ROC). It proves the existence of the company and must be disclosed along with any submission made to the ROC under the Company's Act of 2013.	• Name of the company • Address of the company • Details of the registered office of the company • Director Identification number (DIN) • Registration number of the company (ROC)
Director Identification Number (DIN)	It is a number allotted to any individual that takes up the directorship of any company.	• Name of the DIN holder • Address of the DIN holder • List of directorships held by the DIN holder
Permanent Account Number (PAN)	It is a number that reveals business card information on the holder. The holder may be an individual, a family or a corporate. All entities that file income tax returns must hold a PAN	• Name of the holder • Date of birth/date of incorporation of the holder • Name of the holder's father in case of individual • Signature of the holder in case of individual • Photograph of the holder in case of individual
Aadhaar Number	It is a unique identification number issued by the Indian government to every individual resident of India. It captures demographic and biometric information of every resident Indian individual. The number can be used as the sole identification proof for the holder.	• Name of the holder • Photography of the holder • Gender of the holder • Address of the holder • Name of the holder's father • Date of birth of the holder • Biometric information of the holder

SWIFT Code/ Business Identification Code (BIC)	• 4-character bank code • 2-character country code • 2-character location code • 3-character branch code
Legal Entity Identifier (LEI)	• Legal name of the LEI holder • Registered address of the LEI holder • Address of the headquarters of the LEI holder • ROC number of the LEI holder • Legal form of the LEI holder • Name of the direct parent of the LEI holder • Percentage of shares held by the direct parent • Start date of relationship with the direct parent • Name of ultimate parent • Percentage of shares held by the ultimate parent • Start dote of relationship with the ultimate parent

Source: Gateway House Compilation; Collated using information from various sources.

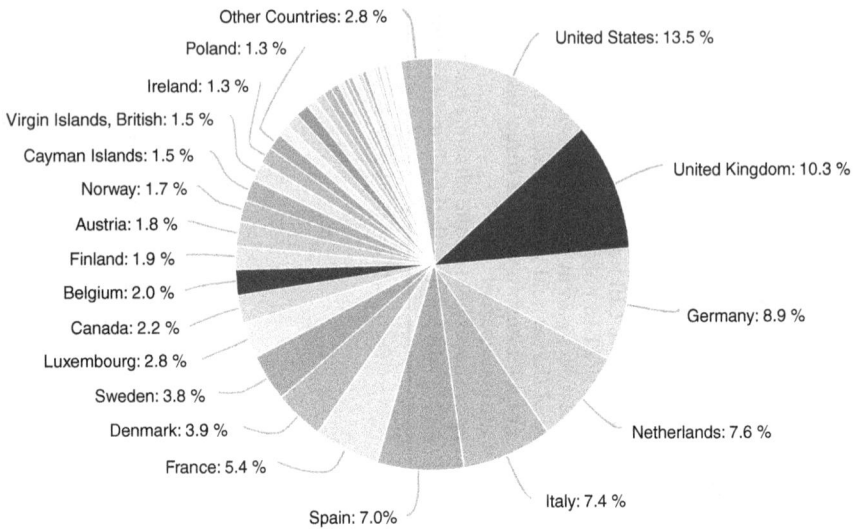

Figure 3.1 LEI adoption by country.
Source: GLEIF LEI Statistics.

However, countries like India, South Korea and Mexico have only one LOU that is overwhelmed by a large number of applications.

The LEI implementation process today is functioning at an optimal pace despite its complexities. Like everything good, global practitioners and industry experts expect the system to crystallise in three years after which it will be possible to trace an entire chain of ownership structures, using the LEI, increasing transparency in cross-border financial transactions.

To enhance the efficacy of the LEI, a global framework is required. In a policy brief for the G20, Gateway House has proposed such a global framework for sharing, cross-referencing and tracing information on an entity's direct and ultimate parents – known as *beneficial ownership information* – by travelling up and down a series of multi-country cross-border transactions. The LEI can be distinctive in this framework. Using information available on the LEI database, any financial transaction can be studied accurately from one end to another and linkages to fraudulent financial practices can be uncovered. It can help identify the total exposure of one company to another, unveiling possible systemic risks arising out of such linkages.

The hope is that such rigorous and robust verifications can prevent another global financial crisis.

28 February 2019

3.5.3 FATF: global terrorist financing watchdog

By Purvaja Modak, former Researcher, Geoeconomic Studies Programme, Gateway House

After the Pulwama attack of 14 February 2019, Pakistan has come under the international scanner for its support and financing of terrorist groups. At a meeting of the FATF in Paris last week, it was pulled up for its inability to choke terrorist financing. This primer illustrates the role of the FATF in tackling terrorist financing and money-laundering and studies its recent review of Pakistan.

3.5.3.1 What is the FATF?

Established in 1989 by the G7 group of countries, the FATF is an inter-governmental body that sets standards for implementing regulatory, legal and operational measures that will combat money laundering and terrorist financing activities.

3.5.3.2 Membership and funding

The FATF is made up of, and funded by, its 36 member countries and two regional organisations, the Gulf Cooperation Council and the European Commission. Pakistan is a full member of the FATF. Indonesia and Saudi Arabia have observer status along with 23 international organisations that have, among other functions, a specific anti-money laundering mission or function. These include the IMF, World Bank, Interpol and the UN.

3.5.3.3 FATF's role

The FATF sets standards, policies, measures on money laundering and financing of terrorist activities and issues guidelines on the reporting of suspicious transactions, freezing of terrorist assets and confiscation of the proceeds of crime.

3.5.3.3.1 FATF'S FAMOUS 40

The FATF's famous 40 standards were developed in 1990 and have been revised periodically since 1996, the most recent being in October 2018. These include

- highlighting the need to enhance transparency by making the beneficial ownership information of legal persons and arrangements accessible (For India, this has implications for curbing tax evasion and black money.);
- listing out the powers and responsibilities of competent authorities like regulators, supervisors and law enforcement agencies (In India, this requires strengthening regulatory agencies like the securities and banking regulators SEBI and RBI, investigative agencies like the CBI, and judges.);
- calling on countries to take immediate steps to ratify and fully implement extant global and regional conventions (like the Vienna Convention) and conventions undergoing negotiations with respect to corruption and money laundering, terrorist financing and cybercrimes.

3.5.3.4 Organisational structure and leadership

The FATF is led by a president, an appointee from one of the member countries who has a year-long tenure. The president heads the FATF secretariat, which is tasked with organising meetings, preparing policy papers and assessment reports. The FATF Secretariat is based in Paris at the headquarters of the OECD.

The current 2018–2019 president of the FATF is Marshall Billingslea of the United States Treasury. The vice president is Xiangmin Liu of the People's Bank of China.

The FATF hosts three, all-member plenary sessions a year. It conducts review meetings, such as the one held on 22 February 2019, to craft action plans for countries to implement the AML/CFT measures and review the progress made. It also holds private sector consultations and meets out of session if required.

3.5.3.5 The FATF and the G20[21]

The G20 is the preeminent body on global economic governance, comprising 20 developed countries and emerging market economies. It represents 85% of the world's GDP and 65% of its population.

The FATF submits a yearly report to the G20, highlighting the activities and initiatives it has undertaken during the year to implement its standards.

On its part, the G20 calls on the FATF to prepare reports based on specific issues related to anti-money laundering and terrorist financing. For example, under the Argentine Presidency of the G20 in 2018, the FATF prepared a report for the G20 on how its anti-money laundering standards apply to crypto-assets.

The G20 countries also make individual and collective commitments to the full and effective implementation of the FATF's standards. In its G20 Leaders' declaration of December 2018, the G20 committed to "regulate crypto-assets for anti-money laundering and countering the financing of terrorism in line with FATF standards" and to "step up efforts in fighting terrorist and proliferation financing, and money laundering."

3.5.3.6 Non-compliance with FATF

Non-compliance with FATF means economic isolation for countries. Punitive measures begin with putting countries on a "watch" list: a grey watch list for countries that have been partially compliant, and the black list for those which are delinquent. The result: denial of access to international banking networks, including multilateral and bilateral development funds.

A consistent blacklister is North Korea. Iran has been on and off the black list and is now on the grey list and so is Pakistan.

3.5.3.7 FATF and Pakistan[22]

Pakistan has already been on FATF's grey list from 2012 to 2015 and is now back on the grey list for non-compliance with its FATF commitments.

On 22 February 2019, as part of its ongoing review of compliance with its standards, the FATF reviewed the progress of 11 countries, including Pakistan, which had anti-money laundering and terrorist financing deficiencies. The goal was to have concrete action plans to enable expeditious compliance within the proposed timeframes. Another review will take place in the coming months.

In June 2018, Pakistan had made a commitment to comply with FATF's standards and while it took some measures, it did not fulfil its obligations, especially those on the risks posed by the financing of terrorist groups like Da'esh, Al Qaeda, Jamaat-ud-Dawa,

Lashkar-e-Taiba, Jaish-e-Mohammad, Haqqani Network and persons affiliated with the Taliban. Since Pakistan did not meet the FATF deadline of January 2019, the FATF retained Pakistan on the "grey" list. However, it did not accede to a recommendation by India to blacklist Pakistan for its terrorist financing activities.

The next deadline for Pakistan is May 2019. If it fails to meet its obligations, it risks being blacklisted by the FATF, effectively shutting down its access to international banking networks. Other punitive measures include targeted financial sanctions in accordance with United Nations Security Council Resolutions and further economic isolation.

The FATF will urge member countries to close existing branches, subsidiaries and representative offices of Pakistani banks that operate in its member countries and terminate all correspondent banking relationships with Pakistani banks. The FATF will advise foreign banks to withdraw their presence from Pakistan. Its sovereign credit ratings will be further downgraded and the country will be unable to access funds from multilateral development banks and international markets. Significantly, Pakistan will also be forced to reveal the safely guarded details of some projects under the China Pakistan Economic Corridor.

One way for Pakistan to get around FATF is the ancient money route of *hawala*, a fund transfer system that exists outside the formal financial system. FATF's scrutiny does not cover *hawala* transactions.

India is once again pressing to put Pakistan on the black list. After the Pulwama attack, on 22 February 2019, India presented evidence to the FATF that reveals links between Pakistani agencies and the Jaish-e-Mohammad, which has taken responsibility for the attack, including funding support.

India will be supported by the United States, Britain, France and Germany, which took the early lead on putting Pakistan on the grey list. But there will surely be opposition from China, Pakistan's all-weather friend and countries of the Gulf Cooperation Council, Turkey and Russia.

Notes

1 https://www.gatewayhouse.in/t20-mumbai-keynote-by-dr-raghuram-rajan/
2 https://www.gatewayhouse.in/t20-mumbai-keynote-by-arvind-panagariya/
3 https://www.gatewayhouse.in/t20mumbai2017/
4 https://www.gatewayhouse.in/interview-shaktikanta-das/
5 https://www.gatewayhouse.in/keynote-gitesh-sarma/
6 https://www.gatewayhouse.in/introductory-remarks-suresh-prabhu/

7 PM Modi's speeches are not available publicly, so this section provides the Briefings provided by the Official spokesperson and/or the G20 Sherpa; where they are available, e.g. 2018 and 2020, it is in point form and reproduced here.
8 https://archivepmo.nic.in/drmanmohansingh/speech-details.php?nodeid=728
9 https://www.mea.gov.in/media-briefings.htm?dtl/24202/Transcript+of+-Media+Briefing+on+forthcoming+G20+Summit+November+6+2014
10 https://www.mea.gov.in/interviews.htm?dtl/26042/Transcript+of+Media+Briefing+by+Official+Spokesperson+and+Sherpa+G20+in+Antalya+November+16+2015
11 No speech, or MEA Briefing is available. This reference is from pg. 11 of the MEA record of the PM's visit to China for the G20 summit: http://www.mea.gov.in/Images/attach/lu5181_05_04_2017_en.pdf
12 https://mea.gov.in/media-briefings.htm?dtl/28731/Media+Briefing+in+Hamburg+on+G20+Summit+Uncorrected+translation+July+08+2017
13 https://www.narendramodi.in/nine-point-agenda-suggested-by-india-to-g-20-for-action-against-fugitive-economic-offences-and-asset-recovery--542472
14 https://mea.gov.in/media-briefings.htm?dtl/31463/Transcript+of+Media+Briefing+by+G20+Sherpa+on+visit+of+Prime+Minister+to+Japan+to+attend+G20+Summit+June+21+2019
15 https://www.gatewayhouse.in/t20-opening-statement-by-dr-burak-akcapar-ambassador-of-turkey-to-india/
16 https://www.gatewayhouse.in/interview-pedro-villagra-delgado/
17 https://www.gatewayhouse.in/fintech-for-the-g20/ - _ftnref1
18 https://www.gatewayhouse.in/lei-financial-transparency/
19 https://www.gatewayhouse.in/lei-financial-transparency/ - _ftn11
20 https://www.gatewayhouse.in/lei-financial-transparency/ - _ftn21
21 https://www.gatewayhouse.in/fatf-terrorist-financing-watchdog/
22 https://www.gatewayhouse.in/fatf-terrorist-financing-watchdog/

Multimedia references

The T20: demystifying the processes

2016: Akshay Mathur in China: https://www.gatewayhouse.in/t20-thinking-g20/
2017: Akshay Mathur in Mumbai on German Presidency: https://www.gatewayhouse.in/t20-mumbai-perspectives-on-the-emerging-world-economy/
2018: Akshy Mathur on Argentina: https://www.gatewayhouse.in/t20-buenos-aires/
2019: Purvaja Modak on Japan and the T20: https://www.gatewayhouse.in/t20-2019-japan/

The G20: issues on the table

2016: The Hangzhou Action Plan, Anoop Singh, https://www.gatewayhouse.in/developing-the-hangzhou-action-plan/
2016: Seeking Structural Reform and Financial Safety, Huang Wei https://www.gatewayhouse.in/structural-reforms-key-objectives-chinas-g20/

2016: Between Germany and China, Claudia Schmucker https://www.gateway-house.in/accent-remains-growth/
2017: Under the German Umbrella, Akshay Mathur https://www.gateway-house.in/t20-mumbai-perspectives-on-the-emerging-world-economy/
2019: Cyber Security Should be Serious, Sameer Patil https://www.gateway-house.in/cyber-security-g20-priority/
2019: Working on Infrastructure with Japan, Suresh Reddy: https://www.gatewayhouse.in/india-japang20/
2019: Japan's G20 Priorities, Naoyuki Yoshino, Dean, ADBI https://www.gatewayhouse.in/realising-japan-g20/
Hideki Asari, Charges d'Affaires ad Interim, Embassy of Japan https://www.gatewayhouse.in/japans-priorities-g20/

The four gateway house policy briefs:

Specific policy proposals to the G20

1 Mainstreaming Natural Capital Valuation
By Purvaja Modak, Akshay Mathur, K. N. Vaidyanathan. *Policy brief for Japan's G20 Presidency, 2019: Purvaja Modak, Akshay Mathur. Encouraging the development and adoption of processes and methods that can quantify the costs of using natural resources.* Read more https://www.gatewayhouse.in/mainstreaming-natural-capital-valuation/
2 A global framework for tracing Beneficial Ownership
By K.N. Vaidyanathan, Akshay Mathur, Purvaja Modak. *Policy brief for Argentina's G20 Presidency, 2018: Proposing policy recommendations for transparency in cross-border financial transactions.* Read more https://www.gatewayhouse.in/a-global-framework-for-tracing-beneficial-ownership/
3 A decentralised, consumer-driven model for the solar eco-system
By Amit Bhandari, Akshay Mathur, Purvaja Modak. *Policy Brief for Germany's G20 Presidency, 2017: The transition to renewable energy is hampered by the lack of suitable, affordable products and specialised financing for its infrastructure. This brief outlines an ecosystem to overcome these hurdles.* Read more https://www.gatewayhouse.in/consumer-driven-model-for-solar/
4 Measuring cross-border trade in services by trading partner country and company
By Akshay Mathur, Purvaja Modak. *Policy brief for Germany's G20 Presidency. The challenge of data classification when it comes to cross-border trade in services.* Read more https://www.gatewayhouse.in/measuring-cross-border-trade-in-services/

4   India's G20 agenda for 2023

Some suggestions

*Sameer Patil, Ambika Khanna, Sanjay
Anandaram (iSpirt), Amit Bhandari
and Chaitanya Giri*

4.1 Introduction

India can choose to use its G20 year wisely – or not. It can make it a
forgettable year of mere event management, as it did with its BRICS
Presidency in 2016, or it can view it as a high cause, a chance to use
the years of 2021 and 2022 to bring itself up to minimum international
standards on physical and virtual infrastructure, quality services,
strong and independent regulation and innovative business models –
as China did with the Olympics in 2008 and with the G20 Presidency
in 2016.

For this, India has to plan ahead and choose what it wants to champion. Below are some suggestions, which play to the country's existing strengths and long-term ambitions, as also to global issues and
agendas – the Digital Economy, Energy Markets and Trading Systems, the International Financial System and the Global Commons.
These will provide an international dimension to India's own Vision
2030, which aims to make India "a modern, technology-driven, high
growth, equitable and transparent society."[1]

4.2 Global digital economy: cyber, tax, fintech

4.2.1 Cyber security

Continuing the G20's digital agenda: In 2016, the G20 leaders' summit
at Hangzhou, China, created the Digital Economy Task Force to propose a common understanding, principles and key areas for development and cooperation in the digital space.[2] The task force focused on
its core agenda of bridging the digital divide, on innovation and promoting investment in information and communication technologies.

DOI: 10.4324/9781003152903-4

The Saudi G20 Presidency of 2020 added cyber security to the digital agenda and made it a priority under the Digital Economy Task Force. In February 2020, it convened the G20 Cybersecurity dialogue, where participants from the government and industry discussed ways to strengthen security, particularly for the micro-, small- and medium-sized enterprises.

India can enhance the discussion by including critical financial infrastructure – the financial markets, intermediaries and now, the fintech platforms that are the base of all economies.

It will serve India's internal goals as well. India has an ambitious target of becoming a $1 trillion digital economy by 2025.[3] At the heart of this target are critical financial infrastructure, digital payment systems, which need uninterrupted functioning and resilience to cyber threats. Innovation also depends on the security of digital economy.[4] These financial institutions and digital payment systems are being targeted globally by state and non-state actors, who are netting the cyber-crime proceeds. India too has been subject to these attacks. The global community's response is mired in silos of jurisdiction and sovereignty.

Hence, India's proposal can provide focus and direction on this, at the G20, during its presidency year. An early start can be made by

- formulating a common definition of critical financial infra-structure since countries define it differently based on their risk perception;
- encouraging member-states to voluntarily offer best practices to secure networks through hardware specifications, information security practices for the workforce and third-party vendors and supply chain management.

Some G20 members such as Japan and Singapore have already offered their national practices on critical infrastructure protection during the G20 meetings. The Digital Economy Task Force can study these, and similar guidelines can be developed for critical financial infrastructure.

4.2.2 Digital tax

Digital tax has been at the core of the G20's digital agenda since 2019. This is because the current international taxation framework serves only the traditional brick-and-mortar businesses and has several loop-holes that are leveraged by digital businesses to evade taxes. Primar-ily, the present framework does not adequately provide for taxing the income of businesses that participate in the economy of a country without a physical presence in its territory. This is particularly the case with digital players like Facebook, Google, Amazon and Netflix, which often use low-tax jurisdictions such as Ireland and Luxembourg to book profits. This is considered unfair business practice, leading to loss of tax revenue to the market country.

India, a huge market for digital players – especially since China is closed to global digital companies – and into which multinationals like Amazon, Facebook and Google have invested about $20 billion in 2020 alone, is especially vulnerable to such tax losses. It is, therefore, directly impacted by the global rules on digital tax.

With the accelerated growth of domestic and cross-border online businesses along with emerging new technologies, a uniform international taxation regime is critical. The G20 and OECD-led BEPS (Base Erosion and Profit Sharing) framework has made two tax proposals on digital taxation in October 2019, which is currently under consideration:

- "Pillar one" is the re-allocation of taxing rights, which addresses where tax should be paid and on what basis.
- "Pillar two" focuses on a global anti-base erosion mechanism, which will prevent profit-shifting and ensure a minimum level of tax to be paid by multinational enterprises.

India has already affirmed its commitment to adhere to the digital tax rules being worked upon by the OECD, as have many other countries.

As a group, the G20 countries are aware of the need for a digital tax to enable a level playing field for markets and participants. The EU is leading the G20's digital tax agenda. France, Spain and the United Kingdom have unilaterally amended their laws to tax global technology giants. In 2016 and 2020, respectively, India introduced an equalisation levy tax and a tax on foreign billings for digital services provided in the country. The China Securities Regulatory Commission has recommended the imposition of digital tax on its technology companies.

However, it is the United States, where the global technology giants are headquartered, which has been stalling the efforts of countries and multilateral to impose a digital tax.

The G20 and OECD had expected some decisions to be made by the end-2020, but COVID-19 led to delays. The decision on their proposals is now expected by mid-2021. Should the G20 and OECD be able to establish consensus and frame rules on digital tax this year as expected, then there may not be much left for India to do in 2023 when it takes over the presidency. Should the decision be delayed or become further embattled when India joins the G20 Troika in 2022, and through its presidency in 2023, it will be well positioned to lead efforts for a consensus-based solution on digital tax including the framing and implementation of uniform international rules, which will replace the unilateral measures undertaken by countries. Consensus being key, the primary aim should be to arrive at a global minimum tax rate, based on the recommendations of the OECD.

4.2.3 Digital public goods

India is pioneering digital public platforms for governance. These are created by the government as a public good, permitting private sector innovation atop. It has been transformational for governance and society, given India's diversity and lack of physical infrastructure, and has attracted the attention from all global quarters including the G20 and the UN, individual governments, philanthropies, academics and the private sector.

These platforms have been developed by volunteers who have built the backbone and tools for financial and technology governance in India. It is designed for scale and diversity. That, combined with the world's cheapest data rates, has made India the world's second largest digitised citizenry,[5] with 1.2 billion IDs, 500 million smartphone users transacting financially, 400 million new bank account holders and adding 100 million every year. It has already overtaken the credit card market globally, with 2 billion transactions in October alone. It's formalising a predominantly informal economic system.

The biggest success is India Stack, the backbone of India's payment and identity systems, the most unique, comprehensive and diverse in the world. Paperless, cashless, presence-less delivery of services across a range of use cases in a low-cost, high-efficiency manner. It is applicable and replicable across the developing and developed world and is being used across sectors – healthcare, post the pandemic; finance; consumer credit.[6, 7]

Key successes:

- **Finance**: The Bank of International Settlement case study of India Stack says India's digital financial infrastructure offers a blueprint for all – efficient and cost-effective and a public good.

- **Healthcare**: Healthstack currently being used in India, a model for other countries to manage post-COVID conditions. Can enable ease of global collaboration on COVID.
- **Consumer credit**: private companies like Bajaj Finserv have built their businesses on India Stack, and are able to process consumer loans in under five minutes – the fastest in the world. Similar experiments are being done with remittances.

It can be a key agenda item for India to add to the G20's Digital Economy Task Force.

- Develop a shared understanding of using digital public platforms as public goods for societal transformation.
- Collaborate on developing Centres of Excellence, Frameworks (Legal, Security, Privacy, Data, e-commerce policy, cross-border data flows) that encourage public-private partnerships for bilateral, regional and global markets. For example, India-Japan working together in Africa.
- Sovereign wealth funds and pension funds can fund initiatives that foster private sector innovation riding on digital public platforms.
- Realities of State capacity in the non-WEIRD world; India's experiences can be beneficial. (WEIRD: Western Educated Industrialized Rich Democratic).

4.3 Global energy markets and trading systems

The Saudi G20 Presidency flagged off the importance of uninterrupted flow of energy while promoting open, competitive and free international energy markets. However, the global pandemic of 2020 has resulted in a transformed energy environment. India, a major importer of energy, and seeking energy independence and security, can place an energy and environment agenda for the G20 during its presidency year, reflecting the new era.

The agenda has three elements: the creation of new benchmarks, new technologies and materials and climate change.

1 **New benchmarks**: The volatility in energy prices, especially the negative oil prices seen early in 2020, will hurt producers and consumers in the long run. Negative prices have also revealed that benchmarks like Brent, nearly four decades old, are now inadequate for price discovery. The G20's goal of "open, competitive

and free energy markets" then will require new price benchmarks for oil and other forms of energy, reflecting the changed global demand-supply patterns – the shift of energy markets from West to Asia, from supply to demand. India can lead the push for new benchmarks, given its status as a major Asian energy consumer, and its free, open and transparent markets.

2 **New technologies and materials**: The pandemic of 2020 has shown that unforeseen disruptions need to be factored into energy markets. There is an increasing push for new technologies such as renewable energy and electric vehicles, which are necessary for the diversification of energy sources. Several G20 countries like Germany and Japan are eliminating fossil fuels like coal and oil from their energy portfolios completely and switching to renewables and battery-powered energy. These nascent technologies are unlikely to provide uninterrupted flows amid major disruptions, like the Corona-19 virus of 2020. The free supply of critical minerals such as lithium, cobalt and rare earths may not continue, given fraught geopolitics. India can lead the efforts for new energy diversification, by exploring other promising clean technologies, such as Hydrogen fuel, starting in its Troika year in 2022, to achieve some success during its presidency year in 2023.

3 **Climate change**: The G20 Leader's Declaration of 2020 endorses the Circular Carbon Economy (CCE) Platform, based on the 4Rs (Reduce, Reuse, Recycle and Remove) framework. CCE looks at managing emissions across all sectors, including, but not limited to energy. This broader approach can be taken further. The recent worldwide push for certain promising technologies – renewable energy and electric vehicles are prime examples – has taken over the discourse on the environment and most of the research and venture funding. In order to avoid focusing all climate change efforts on one set of technologies, the G20 can explore mechanisms to direct funding towards other promising technologies, creating more options to mitigate the risk of climate change. India can lead the G20's Climate Sustainability Working Group efforts to ensure that a monopoly of these new and limited minerals does not become a geopolitical tool in the hands of members.

4.4 International financial system

The international financial system needs an overhaul, and there are several initiatives within the G20 for this. Countries like India have begun to play a significant role, especially with issues that have a domestic and global overlap, such as black money with beneficial ownership, terrorism financing and digitalisation of finance.

With India's strong financial system, strengthened by digital initiatives, the country's policymakers can make bolder moves. A sample of suggestions is below, for the G20 and B20 sub-forum, particularly within the troika of Italy-Indonesia-India, which share many common concerns.

4.4.1 Breaking the oligopoly of rating agencies

The G20 has been effective in keeping the global financial system stable during the COVID-19 crisis year of 2020 – as effective as it was in keeping global financial stability after the 2008 crisis. As Sanjeev Sanyal, Principal Economic Advisor, Government of India, said at Gateway House on 14 January 2021, a year after COVID-19 struck,

> the financial markets have revived, financial flows are taking place, some emerging markets have slowed but there has been no breakdown, goods trade and online services are still alive, lots of shared information and now coordination with the vaccine.[8] The G20 can take credit for it, based on the Global Action Plan put together by the Framework Working Group.

While Sanyal, the 2020 co-chair of the Framework Working Group, acknowledges that global standards set by the G20, including Basel norms for financial systems, are helpful, their uniformity can pose a problem. For instance, capital requirements for banks and financial institutions worldwide are based on a country's credit rating. During a crisis, every country's rating is hit, requiring banks to set aside more capital, when they should be lending.

For emerging markets, he says, this can lead to a crisis. So, in 2020, India worked with the Financial Stability Board and the Bank of International Settlements to reconsider the rules, making them more adaptable to different sovereign conditions.

That effort is still ongoing. However, the long-term solution is to include the diversity of criteria laid down by credit rating agencies, and more importantly, the diversity of credit rating agencies, which are currently concentrated in three western geographies, what Sanyal says is "an oligopoly of three western countries."

This is an effort India, with its strengths in financial markets and a sophisticated financial ecosystem, can lead during its G20 Presidency year in 2023.

4.4.2 SMEs

During Turkey's Presidency year, it gave precedence to the Small and Medium Enterprises, which it felt was under-represented when global rules were being made. Worldwide, SME's account for 90% of all business and 50% of employment. For Turkey, SMEs are critical: they make up over 90% of Turkey's businesses, provide nearly 80% of employment and account for 50% of GDP.[9]

In 2015, Turkey launched the World SME Forum (WSF), whose mandate was to "provide advocacy, know-how, and e-knowledge to enable SMEs to better fulfil their potential as an engine of sustainable growth and job creation."[10] In particular, the G20 Action Plan on SME Financing, launched the same year, was to overcome the "Lack of a sound credit infrastructure... one of the major problems in the credit market for SMEs."[11]

For countries like Italy too, based largely on SMEs and family business, the pandemic year resulted in vast vulnerabilities. According to the OECD, SMEs contribute 67% to Italy's non-finance economy, more than the EU's 56% average, 78% of employment (over the EU's 66%).[12]

Despite several measures, including National Guarantee Fund and co-insurance systems, Italy's SME sector has been badly hit. Marco Felisati, Italy's B20 Sherpa, speaking at Gateway House on 14 February 2021, said Italy would put a focus on export credit and insurance for SMEs.[13]

This is a contribution that the B20 can carry forward during the Italy-Indonesia-India troika year, which India can continue to champion during its presidency year. Businesses in India have had minimal participation in the G20; successfully leading SME recovery and growth will be the ideal platform for them to begin active engagement with the G20.

4.5 Global commons (space and oceans)[14]

The G20 nations are the top drivers of scientific and commercial activities in the global commons of space and oceans. Many developing countries outside this multilateral, from Africa, South America, Eastern Europe and Asia and Oceania, seek to participate in the global commons by offering their natural and human resources in return for cost-effective space services and upgradation of their environmental and socio-economic indicators and national infrastructure.

The initiation of the Space20 by the Saudi Presidency has taken a step forward in this direction.

The Space20 is certainly not the first forum where space agencies of the G20 nations have collaborated. The UNOOSA, United Nations Committee on the Peaceful Use of Outer Space (UNCOPUOS), Space Frequency Coordination Group (SFCG), Inter-Agency Debris Coordination Committee (IADC), Coordination Group on Meteorological Satellites (CGMS), International Astronautical Federation (IAF), Committee on Space Research (COSPAR), International Space Exploration Co-operation Group (ISECG), International Astronomical Union (IAU) – these bring the space agencies together annually or more frequently for various cooperation efforts.

However, the Space20 can carve a niche for itself if it focuses on the wider aspects of "space economy" as it will be a natural extension of the G20's original global finance-economics purview.

India has privatised its space sector in 2020. This has begun to see entrepreneurial success – which can have a demonstration effect, especially in other developing countries. India is a vital link between the developed and the developing world – and can enhance that role in its G20 year. With cost-effective, socio-economically relevant and prudent global commons (space and oceanic) activities, India can lead by sharing its experiences and championing the democratisation of global commons.

In specific to the Space20, India can urge G20 members to:

- share space-based meteorological and earth-observation datasets for the attainment of Nationally Determined Contributions pledged to the UN Paris Agreement
- increase the ambits of the International Civil Aviation Organization to include civilian and commercial sub-orbital and space-transportation
- develop sectoral co-operation within the fifth generation plus (5G+) satellite-based broadband internet services and telecommunications global industry

Notes

1 Press Information Bureau, 'Government Unveils Vision for the Next Decade,' *Ministry of Finance, Government of India.* 02 11, 2019. https://pib.gov.in/newsite/PrintRelease.aspx?relid=187925 (accessed 01 20, 2021).

2 G20 Digital Economy Development and Cooperation Initiative, *G20 Information Centre*, 09 5, 2016. http://www.g20.utoronto.ca/2016/160905-digital.html

3 "India's Trillion-Dollar Digital Opportunity," *Ministry of Electronics and Information Technology.* https://www.meity.gov.in/writereaddata/files/india_trillion-dollar_digital_opportunity.pdf (accessed 03 21, 2020).

4 Carin, Barry. "G20 Safeguards Vulnerabilities of Digital Economy, with Financial Sector Focus." *G20 Insights.* 12 10, 2020. https://www.g20-insights.org/policy_briefs/g20-safeguards-vulnerabilities-digital-economy-financial-sector-focus/ (accessed 01 20, 2021).

5 Pai, T.V. Mohandas and Holla, Nisha. "India's Pioneering Tech-enabled Governance Model". 06 6, 2020. https://www.sundayguardianlive.com/business/indias-pioneering-tech-enabled-governance-model (accessed 01 20, 2021).

6 During the lockdown, migrants from the informal economy were able to receive cash benefits and gain access to food grain. Soon, portable ration cards will enable anyone with a ration card to access rations from any shop in any state in the country, thanks to the India Stack model being extended to all other areas of public engagement, including credit, healthcare, bill payments, eTolls, etc., for across the board use by citizens, commerce (MNCs and MSMEs) and states.

7 https://www.g20-insights.org/policy_briefs/digital-inclusion-strategies-for-the-g20-lessons-in-public-private-cooperation-from-india-and-africa/

8 'G20's future – Italy, Indonesia, India', *Gateway House – Konrad Adenauer Stiftung,* 01 14, 2021. https://www.gatewayhouse.in/events/g20s-italy-indonesia-india/

9 Başçi, Sıdıka and Durucan, Ayşegül. "A Review of Small and Medium Sized Enterprises (SMEs) in Turkey." *Yildiz Social Science Review.* 12 25, 2017. https://www.researchgate.net/publication/322437518_A_Review_of_Small_and_Medium_Sized_Enterprises_SMEs_in_Turkey#:~:text=SMEs%20play%20a%20very%20important, sustainable%20and%20balanced%20economic%20growth (accessed 01 20, 2021).

10 Sahbaz, Ussal. "Turkish Government Launches World SME Forum as Part of Its G20 Strategy." *International Chamber of Commerce.* 05 27, 2015. https://iccwbo.org/media-wall/news-speeches/turkish-government-launches-world-sme-forum-as-part-of-its-g20-strategy/ (Accessed 01 20, 2021.).

11 GPFI, "G20 Action Plan on SME Financing Implementation Framework." *Global Partnership for Financial Inclusion.* 09 16, 2016. https://www.gpfi.org/publications/g20-action-plan-sme-financing-implementation-framework#:~:text=By%20endorsing%20the%20G20%20Action, through%20an%20enabling%20regulatory%20environment (accessed 01 20, 2021).

12 OECD Policy Briefs. "Italian Regional SME Policy Responses." *OECD Trento Centre for Local Development of the OECD Centre for Entrepreneurship, SMEs, Regions and Cities (CFE),* pp. 4–5, 04 22, 2020. https://read.oecd-ilibrary.org/view/?ref=132_132736-237r9rskhm&title=Italian-regional-SME-policy-responses (accessed 01 20, 2021).

13 Felisati, Marco. "Speech Delivered on a Webinar 'G20's Future – Italy, Indonesia, India." *Gateway House – Konrad Adenauer Stiftung.* 01 14, 2021. https://www.gatewayhouse.in/events/g20s-italy-indonesia-india/

14 Giri, Chaitanya. "India Must Back Developing World in Space20." *Gateway House,* 10 26, 2020. https://www.gatewayhouse.in/india-space20/ (accessed 01 18, 2021).

5 Preparing India for the G20 Presidency

5.1 Rule-taker to rule-maker[1]

In 2023, India will be host to the G20, or Group of 20 nations, the world's most influential economic multilateral forum.

The current G20 leaders-level dialogue came into being during the Western financial crisis of 2008 when the G8 countries invited the leaders of the large developing economies, including India and China, to help power their way out of the crisis.

For countries like India, the G20 is a unique global institution, where developed and developing countries have equal stature. Here, the latter can display their global political, economic and intellectual leadership on a par with the world's most powerful countries. It is the agenda-setting body that guides the international financial institutions and global standard-setting body that develops and enforces rules of global economic governance.

The G20 has a rotating presidency and secretariat, ensuring that no country dominates the agenda. Instead, the G20 host sets the agenda for the year, wielding vast direct and indirect influence. Managing this process from inception to fruition showcases a country's talent and administrative ability.

This holds both opportunities and challenges for India: the opportunity to set the global economic governance agenda and make it inclusive, and the challenge of taking on the massive task as G20 President in 2023.

Is India ready for this leadership? Does it have a clear global positioning in place to lead an international financial agenda? Does the country's top political leadership have the capacity to lead the G20 year intellectually, financially, managerially and administratively?

At some levels, India is ready. Indian business and industry is becoming a noteworthy competitor globally. The country's domestic

DOI: 10.4324/9781003152903-5

economy is starting to pick up, thanks to serious structural economic reforms undertaken. The central government is economically stronger, and the states are starting to learn about economic independence. This means they will pull their own weight more, making them contributive and structurally more aligned with their global counterparts.

Geopolitically, India is more internationally engaged. But, it is less engaged geoeconomically, with a narrow focus on the World Bank, IMF and WTO issues. The country has much to contribute beyond these multilaterals and that effort can commence with preparations for the G20 Presidency. In addition to the established themes of financial regulation, trade and other topics, India can lead on several issues, most notably on reform of the Bretton Woods institutions, reconfiguration of global financial regulations, design of a new framework for trade in services and digital economy and establishing better cross-border standards for transparency in financial flows.

It is organisationally that India will have challenges, where the country has an infrastructure, management and intellectual gap.

First, a G20 Presidency brings together several global leaders, their attending delegations and independent experts. Unlike the Olympics and more like Davos, this effort is focused on a small but powerful group which expects good airports, accommodation, conference facilities and communications infrastructure all year round.

Second, the president of the G20 is tasked with leading and managing the global economic agenda for the year. These are typically undertaken by the finance ministry and foreign ministry of a country and a special appointee such as G20 Sherpa, and they together act as the secretariat to the G20 Presidency. In India, the ministries have fine officers with this knowledge, but they are overworked and limited by their short tenures in the departments.

"Global economic governance" is no one ministry's mandate but, in fact, involves many. For example, the ministries of commerce, energy and agriculture have deep stakes in the emerging global economic architecture. The banking and securities regulators – Reserve Bank of India and Securities and Exchange Board of India – play a crucial role in contributing to the formulation of global financial regulations. They all have to work as one.

Third, the logistical exercise is monumental and unprecedented for India. While the country has developed the capacity for organising conferences like "Vibrant Gujarat" and "Pravasi Bhartiya Divas" once a year, and during the COVID-19 year conducted many virtual conferences successful, the G20's all-year, nation-wide requirements are more intense, more subtle and more sophisticated. It needs an energetic secretariat to organise over 170 high-level ministerial, sub-ministerial and sub-forum meetings through the year; and at least 50 task forces (including those of the sub-forums, such as those for think tanks or business). Then, there are content management, negotiation and feedback processes and developing and executing the year-long agenda to culmination. The closest experience for India was in 2016, when, as chair of the five BRICS countries, the ministry of external affairs and finance ministry together organised over 100 meetings, with uneven success, in the presidency year.

Fourth, intellectually, India is constrained on capacity. There are virtually no think tanks or academics which specialise in this subject, except some, like Gateway House, which has focused[2] on this since the early days of the G20. It requires deep inter-disciplinary research on issues of the international monetary system, global financial architecture, global trading system, cross-border use of energy and resources and global climate and sustainability commitments – the latter having spilled over to the G20 from the UN's sustainable development agenda.

This limits India to being a passive rule-taker, not a rule-maker or designer of global economic rules. Consequential economic decisions are then driven by the West, and increasingly by China – neither of which are suitable for an India that should be a leading thinker of the new global economic rules.

Hosting a successful G20 Presidency then is a welcome challenge and a fitting aspiration for the country. Preparations must begin in earnest, with an immediate upgradation of domestic intellectual, administrative and physical infrastructure. This will directly benefit the domestic economy through enhanced human capital and increased international economic engagement via trade, business and finance. The government will have to work together with think tanks, business and other civil society organisations to develop an agenda for India's Presidency.

India is a growing emerging economy, but it leads to no global economic forums. As former Reserve Bank governor Raghuram Rajan said at the inauguration of the first Gateway House-led Think 20[3] (an official sub-forum of economic think tanks of the G20) in 2015, "Those who hold the pen, write the rules." The time has come for India, heading into the 75th year of its independence, to both hold the pen *and* write the rules for a more equitable global economics and governance.

5.2 Intellectual, administrative, infrastructural preparations

In preparing for their G20 Presidency year, most countries prepare their **intellectual capacities** in advance. Because the G20 year has a

Table 5.1 G20 summit costs

Year and Location	Budget
2010 Toronto	CAD 715 million
2011 Cannes	EUR 80 million
2013 St Petersburg	RUB 2 billion (USD 62 million)
2014 Brisbane	AUD 500 million
2015 Antalya	USD 500 million
2016 Hangzhou	USD 24 billion
2017 Hamburg	EUR 72.2 million
2018 Buenos Aires	USD 112 million
2023 India[4]	

Source: University of Toronto G20 Centre.[5]

separate and substantial budget, this is the opportunity that leaders use to give a boost to their intellectual capacity. Academia, think tanks and policy experts within the country are brought in to provide ideas, design solutions and execute them, with early capital support. This is done with not only domestic engagement of administrators in government but also their counterparts from around the world. These experts help aggregate the research, analyse the insights and propose recommendations to the G20 leaders.

The specific expertise required is in international economic relations and the formulation of global economic diplomacy, microeconomics, policy design, financial services and analysis, trade, economics especially global macroeconomics and international business. Increasingly, it also involves expertise in technology, especially fintech and currencies.

The country then assigns a specific think tank or group of think tanks and academics to lead this effort.

For instance, in 2015, Turkey nominated the Economic Policy Research Foundation, TEPAV, a leading Turkish think tank to coordinate the activities of the B20 and T20. TEPAV had a 20-member team to provide research and policy support to the G20 Sherpa's office.

These think tanks work with their global counterparts and, together, develop a series of Policy Briefs, which feed into the Leaders' Statement delivered at the Leaders' Summit at the end of the G20 year.[6]

The **budgets allocated** to the institutions leading the research are substantial. For instance, in 2014, Australia designated the Lowy Institute based in Sydney, a leading Australian think tank, to coordinate the T20 activities for the year, with a budget of $4 million for the year.

The year prior, the Russian Presidency created a 40-member team with experts in international economic relations from various think tanks. Collectively, the job of this forum (Russian Presidential Academy of National Economy and Public Administration, Moscow) was to help the Russian G20 Sherpa's office and the B20/T20 sub-forums with briefing research, content management and stewardship of the intellectual discourse. Budget: $3.5 million for the year.

In 2016, China designated three think tanks as the T20 Sherpa – the Institute for World Economics and Politics (IWEP, China Academy of Social Sciences, Beijing); the Shanghai Institute of International Studies, (Shanghai) and the Chongyang Institute for Financial Studies (RDCY, Renmin University of China, Beijing). All had special expertise in international economic relations and multilateral financial institutions. Budget: $TK million.

Administratively, hosting the G20 is a mammoth organisational task. Preparations to develop and execute the year-long agenda to culmination are hectic. During that year alone, the government has to organise over 150 high-level ministerial, sub-ministerial and sub-forum meetings; at least 50 task forces (inclusive of the sub-forums); manage content, negotiation and feedback and finally, bring it together like a symphony.

For India, the biggest challenge will be building **infrastructure**. A G20 Presidency brings together global leaders, their attending delegations including businesses, independent experts. This powerful group expects good airports, accommodation, conference facilities and communications infrastructure. For the four days of the final leadership summit, the culmination of the year's efforts, a city has to be carefully selected, one with the capacity and infrastructure to host a four-day event at scale and a high level.

At the moment, India is still in the process of building its physical infrastructure in transport especially road and rail, as also its convention capacity.

The lack of this was evident during the June 2018 Annual General Meeting of the Asian Infrastructure Investment Bank (AIIB) held in Mumbai. There was no single, appropriate venue to accommodate the 2,000 attendees of the opening session, which was eventually held in an auditorium for performing arts, with screens set up in different locations for delegates to watch virtually.

One reason India was able to swap its original presidency year of 2022 with Indonesia was because of Indonesia's superior and ready convention and tourism infrastructure – ready to receive visitors after being unused for the duration of the pandemic. The large cities of

Table 5.2 List of think tanks providing research support to their own governments

Russia (2013)	Australia (2014)	Turkey (2015)	China (2016)
Russian Presidential Academy of National Economy and Public Administration (Moscow)	Lowy Institute (Sydney)	Economic Policy Research Foundation of Turkey (Ankara)	Institute for World Economics and Politics (China Academy of Social Sciences, Beijing) Shanghai Institute of International Studies (Shanghai) Chongyang Institute for Financial Studies (Renmin University of China, Beijing)

Germany (2017)	Argentina (2018)	Japan (2019)	Saudi Arabia (2020)
Kiel Institute for the World Economy (IfW Kiel) (Kiel) German Development Institute/Deutsches Institut für Entwicklungspolitik (DIE) (Bonn)	Center of Implementation of Public Policy for Equality and Growth (CIPPEC) (Buenos Aires) Argentine Council for International Relations (CARI) (Buenos Aires)	Asian Development Bank Institute (ADBI) (Tokyo) Institute for International Monetary Affairs (IIMA) (Tokyo) The Japan Institute of International Affairs (JIIA) (Tokyo)	King Abdullah Petroleum Studies and Research Centre(KAPSRC) (Riyadh) King Faisal Centre for Research and Islamic Studies (KFCRIS) (Riyadh)

Source: Collated by Gateway House from various sources.

Table 5.3 Total number of G20 meetings, including sub-forums (2014 and 2015)[7]

Turkey 2015 Meetings	Total
G2G Working Group and Study Group meetings	21
G2G ministerial-level meetings	16
G2G Sherpa meetings	4
Seminars and conferences led by the presidency	35
Sub-forum meetings (B20, L20, T20 and W20)	89
G20 and sub-forum (B20, L20, T20, W20, C20 and Y20) summits	7
Total	**172**

Australia 2014 Meetings	Total
G2G Working Group and Study Group meetings	26
G2G ministerial-level meetings	13
G2G Sherpa meetings	4
G2G Joint ministerial and Sherpa meetings	1
Seminars and conferences led by the presidency	15
Sub-forum meetings (B20 and L20)	30
G20 and Sub-forum (B20, L20, C20 and Y20) summits	5
Total	**94**

Source: Collated and analysed by Gateway House, from Ministry of Finance, Government of India.

Table 5.4 List of G20 Working Group meetings held under Turkey's presidency (2015)

Date	Description of Action/ Meeting	Place	Level
20–21 January 2015	Framework Working Group meeting no. 1	Vancouver	WG
29–30 January 2015	Investment and Infrastructure Working Group meeting no. 1	Ankara	WG
2–3 February 2015	Development Working Group meeting no. 1	Istanbul	WG
24–25 February 2015	Energy Sustainability Working Group meeting no. 1	Antalya	WG
26–28 February 2015	Employment Working Group meeting no. 1	Antalya	WG
4–5 March 2015	Anti-corruption Working Group meeting no. 1	Istanbul	WG
23–24 March 2015	Framework Working Group meeting no. 2	Kumarakom, Kerala	WG
9–10 April 2015	Development Working Group meeting no. 2	Ankara	WG

7–9 May 2015	Employment Working Group meeting no. 2	Istanbul	WG
25–26 May 2015	Investment and Infrastructure Working Group meeting no. 2	Singapore	WG
25–26 May 2015	Energy Sustainability Working Group meeting no. 2	Istanbul	WG
28–29 May 2015	Framework Working Group meeting no. 3	Rome	WG
4–5 June 2015	Development Working Group meeting no. 3	Izmir, Turkey	WG
16–17 June 2015	Anti-corruption Working Group meeting no. 2	Washington, DC	WG
23–25 July 2015	Employment Working Group meeting no. 3	Cappadocia, Turkey	WG
27–28 July 2015	Climate Finance Study Group meeting	Ankara	WG
20–21 August 2015	Investment and Infrastructure Working Group meeting no. 3	Berlin	WG
1–3 September 2015	Energy Sustainability Working Group meeting no. 3	Izmir, Turkey	WG
3–4 September 2015	G20 Labour and Employment Ministers' meeting	Ankara	WG
14–16 September 2015	Development Working Group meeting no. 4	Antalya	WG
17–18 September 2015	Framework Working Group meeting no. 4	Seoul	WG
15–16 October 2015	G20 ACWG 3rd meeting	Paris	WG

Source: Gateway House analysis.

Table 5.5 List of G20 Working Group meetings held under Saudi Arabia's presidency (2020)

Date	Description of Action/Meeting	Place	Level
10–11 December 2019	1st Development Working Group Meeting	Riyadh	WG
15–16 December 2019	1st Education Working Group Meeting	Riyadh	WG
18–19 December 2019	1st Infrastructure Working Group Meeting	Riyadh	WG
12–13 January 2020	1st Framework Working Group Meeting	Riyadh	WG
14–16 January 2020	1st Health Working Group Meeting	Riyadh	WG
31 January 2020	1st International Financial Architecture Working Group Meeting	Riyadh	WG

4–6 February 2020	1st Anti-Corruption Working Group Meeting	Riyadh	WG
4–6 February 2020	1st Employment Working Group Meeting	Jeddah	WG
1–3 March 2020	2nd Health Working Group Meeting	Jeddah	WG
3–4 March 2020	1st Climate Stewardship Working Group Meeting	Riyadh	WG
7–8 March 2020	1st Energy Sustainability Working Group Meeting	Riyadh	WG
8–9 March 2020	1st Trade and Investment Working Group Meeting	Riyadh	WG
1 April 2020	1st Exceptional International Financial Architecture Working Group Session	Virtual	WG
6–7 April 2020	1st Tourism Working Group Meeting	Virtual	WG
7 April 2020	2nd Framework Working Group Meeting	Virtual	WG
8 April 2020	2nd Employment Working Group Meeting	Virtual	WG
8 April 2020	2nd Exceptional International Financial Architecture Working Group Session	Virtual	WG
9 April 2020	2nd Infrastructure Working Group Meeting	Virtual	WG
10 April 2020	3rd Exceptional International Financial Architecture Working Group Session	Virtual	WG
17 April 2020	3rd Health Working Group Meeting	Virtual	WG
22 April 2020	Extraordinary Trade and Investment Working Group Meeting	Virtual	WG
14 May 2020	2nd Extraordinary Trade and Investment Ministers Meeting	Virtual	WG
28 May 2020	4th Exceptional International Financial Architecture Working Group Session	Virtual	WG
8 June 2020	3rd Framework Working Group Meeting	Virtual	WG
9 June 2020	3rd Infrastructure Working Group Meeting	Virtual	WG
17–18 June 2020	2nd Development Working Group Meeting	Virtual	WG
23–24 June 2020	2nd International Financial Architecture Working Group Meeting	Virtual	WG
28–29 June 2020	2nd Trade and Investment Working Group Meeting	Virtual	WG

(Continued)

2–3 July 2020	2nd Tourism Working Group Meeting	Virtual	WG
7–8 July 2020	2nd Education Working Group Meeting	Virtual	WG
7–8 July 2020	4th Framework Working Group Meeting	Virtual	WG
20–21 July 2020	2nd Climate Stewardship Working Group Meeting	Virtual	WG
22–23 July 2020	2nd Energy Sustainability Working Group Meeting	Virtual	WG
19–20 August 2020	3rd Employment Working Group	Virtual	WG
1–2 September 2020	3rd Development Working Group Meeting	Virtual	WG
3–4 September 2020	3rd Education Working Group Meeting	Virtual	WG
7–10 September 2020	2nd Anti-corruption Working Group Meeting	Virtual	WG
7–8 September 2020	4th Employment Working Group Meeting	Virtual	WG
10 September 2020	5th Exceptional International Financial Architecture Working Group Session	Virtual	WG
19–21 September 2020	3rd Climate Stewardship Working Group Meeting	Virtual	WG
20–21 September 2020	3rd Trade and Investment Working Group Meeting	Virtual	WG
22 September 2020	3rd International Financial Architecture Working Group Meeting	Virtual	WG
23–25 September 2020	3rd Energy Sustainability Working Group Meeting	Virtual	WG
24 September 2020	5th Framework Working Group Meeting	Virtual	WG
25 September 2020	6th Exceptional International Financial Architecture Working Group Session	Virtual	WG
28 September 2020	4th Infrastructure Working Group	Virtual	WG
6 October 2020	3rd Tourism Working Group Meeting	Virtual	WG
8 October 2020	7th Exceptional International Financial Architecture Working Group Session	Virtual	WG
19–21 October 2020	3rd Anti-Corruption Working Group	Virtual	WG
2 November 2020	6th Framework Working Group Meeting	Virtual	WG
5 November 2020	8th Exceptional International Financial Architecture Working Group Session	Virtual	WG

Source: Collated by Gateway House from various sources.

Table 5.6 List of G20 Sherpa meetings held under Turkey's presidency (2015)

Date	Description of Action/Meeting	Place	Level
15–16 December 2014	Sherpa meeting no. 1	Istanbul	Sherpa
26–27 March 2015	Sherpa meeting no. 2	Izmir	Sherpa
16–17 June 2015	Sherpa meeting no. 3	Bodrum	Sherpa
13–14 October 2015	Sherpa meeting no. 4	Ankara	Sherpa

Source: Collated by Gateway House from various sources, including Ministry of Finance, Government of India.

Table 5.7 List of G20 Sherpa meetings held under Saudi Arabia's presidency (2020)

Date	Description of Action/Meeting	Place	Level
4–5 December 2020	Sherpa meeting no. 1	Riyadh	Sherpa
11–12 March 2020	Sherpa meeting no. 2	Khobar	Sherpa
25 March 2020	Extraordinary Sherpa's meeting no. 1	Virtual	Sherpa
24 July 2020	Extraordinary Sherpa's meeting no. 2	Virtual	Sherpa
29–30 September 2020	Sherpa meeting no. 3		Sherpa
27–29 October 2020	Extraordinary Sherpa's meeting no. 3	Virtual	Sherpa
17–19 November 2020	Sherpa meeting no. 4	Virtual	Sherpa

Source: Collated by Gateway House from various sources.

Mumbai and Delhi are now building large convention spaces, which are expected to be ready in time for a physical G20 meet in 2023.

These are major expenses. China spent an estimated $24 billion for its 2016 G20 Leaders' summit, including readying the city of Hangzhou as host. A year later, Germany budgeted and spent a fraction of that an estimated $90 million for its G20 summit in Hannover.[8]

These massive numbers contracted in 2020, when, under the Saudi Arabian Presidency, the meetings and proceedings of the G20 were held virtually. Expenditure numbers are not available for Saudi Arabia, but the Kingdom's investment in becoming G20-ready would be money well spent, as according to local Saudi investment bank Jadwa Investment, the country was expected to receive a 0.2% boost in non-oil revenues from all the activity around the G20 alone.

Table 5.8 List of G20 Ministerial meetings held under Turkey's presidency (2015)

Date	Description of Action/Meeting	Place	Level
11–12 December 2014	Finance and Central Bank Deputies meeting no. 1	Istanbul	Ministerial
8–9 February 2015	Finance and Central Bank Deputies meeting no. 2	Istanbul	Ministerial
9–10 February 2015	Finance Ministers and Central Bank Governors no. 1	Istanbul	Ministerial
23 March 2015	G20 Agriculture Deputies Meeting	Ankara	Ministerial
16 April 2015	Finance and Central Bank Deputies meeting no. 3	Washington, DC	Ministerial
16–17 April 2015	Finance Ministers and Central Bank Governors no. 2	Washington, DC	Ministerial
6–8 May 2015	G20 Agriculture Ministers Meeting	Istanbul	Ministerial
15–16 June 2015	Finance and Central Bank Deputies meeting no. 4	Bodrum	Ministerial
2–3 July 2015	G20 Agriculture Deputies Meeting	Izmir, Turkey	Ministerial
3–4 September 2015	Finance and Central Bank Deputies meeting no. 5	Ankara	Ministerial
4–5 September 2015	Finance Ministers and Central Bank Governors no. 3	Ankara	Ministerial
4 September 2015	Joint meeting of G20 Finance and Labour and Employment Ministerial meeting	Ankara	Ministerial
29–30 September 2015	G20 Tourism Ministers' meeting (T.20)	Antalya	Ministerial
2 October 2015	G20 Energy Ministers meeting	Istanbul	Ministerial
5–6 October 2015	G20 Trade Ministers meeting	Istanbul	Ministerial
8 October 2015	Finance Ministers and Central Bank Governors Dinner	Peru	Ministerial

Source: Collated by Gateway House from various sources, including from Ministry of Finance, Government of India.

Table 5.9 List of G20 Ministerial meetings held under Saudi Arabia's presidency (2020)

Date	Description of Action/ Meeting	Place	Level
6–7 December 2020	1st Finance and Central Banks' Deputies Meeting	Riyadh	Ministerial
26–27 January 2020	1st Agriculture Deputies Meeting	Riyadh	Ministerial
20–21 February 2020	2nd Finance and Central Banks' Deputies Meeting	Riyadh	Ministerial
22–23 February 2020	1st Finance Ministers and Central Bank Governors Meeting	Riyadh	Ministerial
3–4 March	1st Environment Deputies Meeting	Riyadh	Ministerial
23 March 2020	1st Extraordinary Finance Ministers and Central Bank Governors Meeting	Virtual	Ministerial
30 March 2020	Extraordinary Trade and Investment Ministers Meeting	Virtual	Ministerial
31 March 2020	2nd Extraordinary Finance Ministers and Central Bank Governors Meeting	Virtual	Ministerial
10 April 2020	Extraordinary Energy Ministers Meeting	Virtual	Ministerial
14 April 2020	3rd Finance and Central Bank Deputies Meeting	Virtual	Ministerial
15 April 2020	2nd Finance Ministers and Central Bank Governors Meeting	Virtual	Ministerial
19 April 2020	Health Ministers Meeting	Virtual	Ministerial
21 April 2020	Extraordinary Agriculture Ministers Meeting	Virtual	Ministerial
23 April 2020	Extraordinary Employment Ministers Meeting	Virtual	Ministerial
24 April 2020	Extraordinary Tourism Ministers Meeting	Virtual	Ministerial
30 April 2020	Extraordinary Digital Economy Ministers Meeting	Virtual	Ministerial
13 May 2020	1st Water Deputies Meeting	Virtual	Ministerial
14 May 2020	2nd Extraordinary Trade and Investment Ministers Meeting	Virtual	Ministerial
27 June 2020	Extraordinary Education Ministers Meeting	Virtual	Ministerial
10 July 2020	2nd Water Deputies Meeting	Virtual	Ministerial
13–16 July 2020	2nd Environment Deputies Meeting	Virtual	Ministerial

(Continued)

Date	Description of Action/ Meeting	Place	Level
16–17 July 2020	4th Finance and Central Bank Deputies Meeting	Virtual	Ministerial
18 July 2020	3rd Finance Ministers and Central Bank Governors Meeting	Virtual	Ministerial
22–23 July 2020	Digital Economy Ministers Meeting	Virtual	Ministerial
3 September 2020	Extraordinary G20 Foreign Ministers Meeting	Virtual	Ministerial
5 September 2020	Education Minister's Meeting	Virtual	Ministerial
10–11 September 2020	2nd Agriculture and Water Deputies Meeting	Virtual	Ministerial
10 September 2020	Employment Ministers Meeting	Virtual	Ministerial
12 September 2020	Agriculture and Water Ministers Meeting	Virtual	Ministerial
14–15 September 2020	3rd Environment Deputies Meeting	Virtual	Ministerial
14–16 December 2020	Joint Meeting of G20 Finance and Health Deputies	Virtual	Ministerial
16 September 2020	Environment Ministers Meeting	Virtual	Ministerial
17 September 2020	Joint Meeting of G20 Finance and Health Ministers	Virtual	Ministerial
22 September 2020	Trade Ministers Meeting	Virtual	Ministerial
27–28 September 2020	Energy Ministers Meeting	Virtual	Ministerial
7 October 2020	Tourism Ministers Meeting	Virtual	Ministerial
12–13 October 2020	5th Finance and Central Bank Deputies Meeting	Virtual	Ministerial
14 October 2020	4th Finance Ministers and Central Bank Governors Meeting	Virtual	Ministerial
22 October 2020	Anti-corruption Ministers Meeting	Virtual	Ministerial
22 October 2020	Joint Meeting of G20 Finance and Health Deputies	Virtual	Ministerial
11–12 November 2020	G20 Finance Track Deputies Meeting	Virtual	Ministerial
19 November 2020	The Joint Meeting of Sherpas and Finance Deputies	Virtual	Ministerial
20 November 2020	Finance Ministers Meeting	Virtual	Ministerial

Source: Collated by Gateway House from various sources.

Table 5.10 Total number of sub-forum meetings held under each presidency (2013–2015)

Russia 2013	Sub-forum	No. of meetings
	B20	31
	L20	8
Australia 2014	**Sub-forum**	**No. of meetings**
	B20	26
	L20	6
Turkey 2015	**Sub-forum**	**No. of meetings**
	B20	52
	L20	7
	T20	29
	W20	5

Source: compiled and analysed by Gateway House from various sources, including from Ministry of Finance, Government of India.

But by the time India's turn comes in 2023, the pandemic will have receded, physical meetings will resume and the large budgets will need to be allocated – hopefully with returns in revenue from the G20 activity. So far, a small amount has been allocated: in February 2020, Indian Finance Minister Nirmala Sitharaman allocated the minimal Rs. 100 crores or $13.6 million, to begin the G20 preparations.[9]

A significant allocation of funds for the G20 year is security. Given the high profile of the participants, strict security is required all year round, at all the various G20 venues. In particular, the city where the G20 leaders convene for the summit need additional forces apart from the local police, medical arrangements, venue sanitisation and crowd control, especially with the civil society protests that typically accompany major global events.

5.3 The influence of the host country

The G20 Presidency is significant because of the influence the host country wields on a wide range of global issues. The G20 host **directly influences** the global economic agenda and the negotiation process for the year, and the year preceding and after its presidency as part of the Troika. In addition, it indirectly influences the agenda and proceedings of the sub-forums (B20, T20 and others), and also **indirectly influences** the direction of the work of multilateral institutions such as the IMF, FSB and the World Bank which work closely with the G20 host and member countries.

Directly, the host country sets the vision statement and influences the **global economic agenda** for the year. This permits the host country to design rules and introduce issues for discussion that are of importance to itself. For example, Australia, the 2014 G20 President, put infrastructure on the global agenda because it has domestic corporate strength in infrastructure-building and commodities, and institutional capital to invest in the same. Turkey, the 2016 President, put small and medium enterprises (SMEs) at the centre of its agenda because SMEs are the engine of job creation and inclusive growth everywhere but especially in Turkey.

The host country leads the **negotiation process** to influence the outcome to domestic satisfaction and with global consensus. This is done by formulating and leading the government-led discussions and various task forces.

For instance, in February 2014, Australia had the first meeting of the new Infrastructure and Investment Working Group replacing the International Financial Architecture Working Group. The new group identified how private sector investment can be channelled into infrastructure and medium-sized enterprises. Five of the seven working groups were chaired or co-chaired by Australia.

As is now the norm with multilateral groupings, the G20 President has the prerogative to ask **special invitees** – non-G20 countries – to the full range of government meetings. These are usually countries which have geopolitical significance to the host country.

The G20 rules permit inviting five non-member countries, of which at least two are from Africa.

The international financial institutions have been special invitees to the G20 meetings since 2008. These include the IMF, World Bank and the Financial Stability Board, the WTO, ASEAN, NEPAD and OECD, the Financial Stability Board, International Labour Organisation, IMF, OECD, UN, WTO and FAO.

These institutions have been deeply engaged with the G20 since 2008, and the G20's host country can indirectly influence the research and action agenda of the major multilateral institutions. One way is by directing the multilateral institutions to **initiate research reports** on issues specific to the host country's agenda for that year – because many countries still depend on the research departments of these institutions for technical support.

Besides the Sherpa meeting, and the Finance Minister and Central Bank Governor meetings, the G20 also hosts several **ministerial meetings** on agriculture, energy, tourism and trade. These can be areas of specific interest to the host country and is an opportunity to cross-pollinate ideas with some of the best minds in the world, at the host's home table.

The host country **indirectly influences** the agenda and the proceedings of the various sub-forums like the B20 and T20. It can introduce

Table 5.11 Special country invitees by each presidency (2008–2020)

Mexico 2012	Russia 2013	Australia 2014	Turkey 2015
Spain	Spain	Spain	Spain
Benin (Chair of AU)	Ethiopia (Chair of AU)	Mauritania (Chair of AU)	Zimbabwe (Chair of AU)
Cambodia (Chair of ASEAN)	Brunei (Chair of ASEAN)	Myanmar(chair of ASEAN)	Malaysia (chair of ASEAN)
Ethiopia (NEPAD)	Senegal (NEPAD)	Senegal (NEPAD)	Senegal (NEPAD)
Colombia (representative of Latin America)	Kazakhstan	New Zealand	Azerbaijan
Chile (representative of Latin America)	Singapore	Singapore	Singapore

China 2016	Germany 2017	Argentina 2018	Japan 2019	Saudi Arabia 2020
Thailand	Spain	Spain	The Netherlands	Spain
Spain	Norway	Chile	Spain	Jordan
Kazakhstan	The Netherlands	The Netherlands	Vietnam	Singapore
Singapore	Singapore	Rwanda (President of AU)	Singapore	Switzerland
Egypt	Guinea (President of AU)	Singapore (Chair of ASEAN)	Chile (President of APEC forum)	Vietnam (Chair of ASEAN)
Senegal (NEPAD)	Vietnam (President of APEC)	Senegal (NEPAD)	Senegal (NEPAD)	South Africa (Chair of AU)
Laos (Chair of ASEAN)	Senegal (NEPAD)	Jamaica (CARICOM)	Thailand (Chair of ASEAN)	UAE (Chair of GCC)
Chad (President of AU)			Egypt (President of AU)	Rwanda (NEPAD)

Source: Collated by Gateway House from various sources, including from Ministry of Finance, Government of India.

new sub-fora, as Mexico did, by introducing the T20 in 2012, and Turkey did by introducing the W20 (for women's issues). This gives the home country's institutions the chance to learn how to manage these

Table 5.12 Special institutional invitees by each presidency (2008–2020)

Mexico 2012	Russia 2013	Australia 2014	Turkey 2015	Saudi Arabia 2020
Financial Stability Board	Financial Stability Board	Financial Stability Board	Financial Stability Board	Financial Stability Board
International Labour Organization	International Labour Organization	International Labour Organization	International Labour Organization	International Labour Organization
IMF	IMF	IMF	IMF	
OECD	OECD	OECD	OECD	
United Nations	United Nations	United Nations	United Nations	IMF
World Trade Organization	World Trade Organization	World Trade Organization	World Trade Organization	OECD
World Bank	World Bank	World Bank	World Bank	United Nations
Food and Agriculture Organization				World Trade Organization
				World Bank
				World Health Organization
				Food and Agriculture Organization
				Arab Monetary Fund
				Islamic Development Bank

China 2016	Germany 2017	Argentina 2018	Japan 2019
Financial Stability Board	Financial Stability Board	Financial Stability Board	Financial Stability Board
International Labour Organization	International Labour Organization	International Labour Organization	International Labour Organization
IMF	IMF	IMF	IMF
OECD	OECD	OECD	OECD
United Nations	United Nations	United Nations	United Nations
World Trade Organization	World Trade Organization	World Trade Organization	World Trade Organization
World Bank	World Bank	World Bank	World Bank
	World Health Organization		

Source: Collated by Gateway House from various sources, including from Ministry of Finance, Government of India.

fora, their development and activities, along with their counterparts from around the world.

These fora often become trial balloons for the ideas the host country wants to project. For instance, in 2011, France introduced the idea of having a permanent secretariat for the G20; then, in 2015, in preparation for its 2016 presidency, China proposed the permanent secretariat be established in China, formally testing it with policy experts globally. Thankfully, it was rejected by the G20 leaders who prefer to keep the "leader-led and informal group"[10] character of G20.

In some cases, the host country was able to **introduce a discourse on issues** which was otherwise not high on the G20 agenda. For instance, Turkey co-hosted a conference on migration and development, titled "G20: Global Forum on Migration and Development" with the Global Migration Group (GMG) and the Global Forum on Migration and Development (GFMD) to discuss issues related to remittances and financial inclusion.

5.4 Benefits of hosting the G20 Presidency

The benefits of a G20 Presidency are vast. The president country positions itself as a global economic and political leader for the year and is respected and acknowledged as such. Through its year-long, one-on-one privileged access to heads of state, multilateral institutions, multinational corporations and global events, it is able to showcase its worldview and aspirations as a global problem-solver. This branding is visible when the G20 Presidency co-hosts events at conferences like the World Economic Forum. This often brings dividends in the host's domestic constituency as well.

Hosting the G20 requires an upgrading of domestic intellectual, administrative and physical infrastructure. This then directly benefits the domestic economy through enhanced human capital and increased international economic engagement via trade, business and finance.

The G20 Presidency showcases a country's vision for the year and allows its geopolitical preferences to be visible.

Saudi Arabia used its presidency year to showcase and execute its Vision 2030.[11]

And, India will aim to do the same in 2023, with its Vision 2030, to make India "a modern, technology-driven, high-growth, equitable and transparent society."[12]

In **2014**, **Australia** was able to position itself in the forum as the leader of the (then) Asia Pacific region, specifically representing the interests of the ASEAN, PIF, EAS and APEC nations – a platform usually claimed by the United States and Japan. Australia held special consultative meetings with all these forums.

It also bought its koalas to the Summit, its G20 year earning the phrase "koala diplomacy." However, Australia's leadership played second fiddle to the United States – who can forget the public admonishing of Russian President Vladimir Putin on the Ukraine, compelling him to leave the forum early. Still, even though it was considered undiplomatic, it played well to the domestic Australian audience and with the White House in Washington, DC.

Australia also set up the Global Infrastructure Hub, to work with public and private sectors globally to increase the flow and quality of crucial public infrastructure projects. In particular, it was to share data, knowledge, best practices and insights to facilitate the delivery of G20 members' economic, social and environmental outcomes through better infrastructure. Unfortunately, the follow-up to the Hub was not as aggressive as its promotion, and it has not lived up to its promise.[13]

In **2015**, **Turkey** did better for itself. The Turkey-led B20 established World SME Forum with a focus on inclusion, especially SMEs, which was a global platform to counter-balance the influence of the multinationals on the World Economic Forum.[14]

The economic inequality that gave rise to the Arab uprisings and the migrations from Iraq and Syria motivated Turkey's decision to put inclusion on the agenda. Within Turkey, business groups such as the Union of Chambers and Commodity Exchanges of Turkey (TOBB) have a very strong base of chambers and associations representing small and medium enterprises.

Turkey also hosted multiple seminars with the IMF, the World Bank and the Islamic Development Bank on "Islamic finance." "Islamic finance" is not on the G20 agenda, but it got a legitimate representation under the Turkish Presidency.

As with Islamic finance, Turkey's special country invitee was Azerbaijan, a Central Asian country with which it has a strategic relationship, particularly as a reliable partner for gas.[xi] Azerbaijan's state oil company Socar is one of the largest investors in Turkey. But, Turkey's political relations with Azerbaijan go back even further. Turkey was the first country to recognise Azerbaijan's independence, and it has always leaned in favour of Azerbaijan in its conflict with Armenia – as seen in the 2020 conflict between the two countries. The special invitee status gave exposure to tiny Azerbaijan, which, otherwise, would not have access to this select global economic platform.

In 2016, China provided the first insights into its global trade and tech rule-maker intentions. Under the Chinese Presidency, Jack Ma launched the idea of e-World Trade Platform (SME) called the E-WTP to counter WTO.

In line with this initiative, China developed the city of Hangzhou to host the G20 summit. Hangzhou is home to China's tech giant, Alibaba and some other smaller tech startups.

In a well-synthesised plan, and using its impressive infrastructure-building capacity, China built a major conference venue, new motor ways and residential complexes in Hangzhou, with new trees planted and polluting factories shut down. The estimated cost: $24 billion (though there are no official statistics).[15]

In **2019, Japan** introduced the Osaka track on the Digital Economy at the G20 summit.

Its goal was to finalise international rules for digital trade – the trade-related aspects of electronic commerce at the WTO – drafting rules on data flows, removal of prohibitions on data localisation and cloud computing among others. This would have largely benefitted developed countries like Japan, the United States, the European Union and Singapore.

But several developing countries like India, Indonesia and South Africa did not sign it, citing it as an informal, behind-the-scenes negotiation by some rather than a consensus-based negotiation by all, which is the base of multilateral negotiations.

In **2018, Saudi Arabia** announced that it would set up a space programme to create opportunities and jobs for young Saudis. In October **2020, the Saudi Space** Commission initiated the Space20, the first meeting of the space agency leaders of the G20 countries, to collaborate on existing and future projects – giving its own aspirations a boost.

Notes

1 Mathur, Akshay. "Preparing India for the G20 Presidency in 2022." *Gateway House.* 01 31, 2019. https://www.gatewayhouse.in/india-g20-presidency/ (accessed 01 20, 2021).

2 https://www.gatewayhouse.in/india-g20-presidency/

3 https://www.gatewayhouse.in/t20-mumbai-keynote-by-dr-raghuram-rajan/

4 Rs.100 crore or USD 13.8 million is the amount budgeted for G20 preparation in Union Budget 2020 by Ministry of Finance, Government of India.

5 Muhanna, Duja. "G20 Summit Costs, 2010–2018." *G20 Information Centre, University of Toronto*. 11 28, 2018. http://www.g20.utoronto.ca/factsheets/factsheet_costs-g20.html (accessed 01 20, 2021).
6 Mathur, Akshay, Modak, Purvaja and Bhandari, Amit. "A Decentralized, Consumer-driven Model for the Solar Eco-system. G20 Policy Brief, *G20 Insights*. 04 6, 2017. https://www.g20-insights.org/policy_briefs/decentralized-consumer-driven-model-solar-eco-system/ (accessed 01 19, 2021).
   Vaidyanathan, K.N., Mathur, Akshay and Modak, Purvaja. "Mainstreaming Natural Capital Valuation." G20 Policy Brief, *G20 Insights*. 05 06, 2019. https://www.g20-insights.org/policy_briefs/mainstreaming-natural-capital-valuation/ (accessed 01 18, 2021).
   Vaidyanathan, K.N., Mathur, Akshay and Modak, Purvaja. "A Global Framework for Tracing Beneficial Ownership." G20 Policy Brief, *G20 Insights*. 07 23, 2019. https://www.g20-insights.org/policy_briefs/a-global-framework-for-tracing-beneficial-ownership/ (accessed 01 19, 2021).
   Mathur, Akshay and Modak, Purvaja. "Measuring Cross-border Trade in Services by Trading Partner Country and Company." 04 5, 2017. https://www.g20-insights.org/policy_briefs/measuring-cross-border-trade-services-trading-partner-country-company/ (accessed 01 18, 2021).
7 Full list of meetings for the earlier presidencies available in the Appendix.
8 FAQs about the G20, *G20 Germany 2017*. https://www.g20germany.de/Webs/G20/EN/G20/FAQs/faq_node.html#:~:text=The%202017%20G20%20summit%20cost%20the%20German%20government%20%E2%82%AC%2072.2%20million (accessed 01 20, 2021).
9 "Point 87, Budget Speech by Nirmala Sitharaman, Finance Minister of India." 02 1, 2021. https://www.indiabudget.gov.in/budget2020-21/doc/Budget_Speech.pdf
10 'India and the G20' Private paper by Gateway House for Ministry of Finance, November 2015.
11 https://vision2030.gov.sa/en
12 India Vision 2030: https://pib.gov.in/newsite/PrintRelease.aspx?relid=187925)
13 Global Infrastructure Hub, A G20 Initiative – https://www.gihub.org/
14 World SME Forum http://www.worldsmeforum.org/about/
15 Wang, Yue. "What We Know about China's G20 Host City Hangzhou." *Forbes*. 09 2, 2016. https://www.forbes.com/sites/ywang/2016/09/02/what-we-know-about-chinas-g20-summit-host-city-hangzhou/#228d86e175f7 (accessed 01 20, 2021).
   "'Paradise on Earth': China's Hangzhou Gets Propaganda Facelift for G20 Summit." *The Guardian*. 08 31, 2016. https://www.theguardian.com/world/2016/aug/31/china-hangzhou-propaganda-facelift-g20-summit (accessed 01 20, 2021).

6 G20 today

At the crossroads or marching to success?

Rajiv Bhatia and Manjeet Kripalani

The G20 holds an elevated status: it is often referred to as the world's economic steering committee. It was central to that role in 2008, after the global financial crisis – and it was central again in 2020, the year of the COVID-19 pandemic.

In the 12 years between 2008 and 2020, many wondered if the G20 had lost its way. Terms like mid-life crisis, mission creep and problematic policy cooperation were used for the G20. This criticism may be justified, but it is also harsh. Mulitlateral bodies like the United Nations and its associate systems, formed in 1947, have long needed reform, but not been enabled by member nations, nor wrought it from within. The WTO still does not have a full appellate bench of three required to resolve trade disputes. War and terrorism created a wave of migration especially from West Asia and North Africa, engulfing Europe in a crisis of migration, assimilation and employment. Climate change and sustainable development are embattled. A rising China now has its own bureaucrats at the head of a third of the UN's 15 principal agencies and is rapidly dominating others in what appears to be a strategic takeover of the global multilateral system.

Consequently, in addition to its already loaded financial governance agenda, significant multilateral issues from migration to climate change, environment, trade, culture, security and defence, the UN's sustainable development goals (SDGs), digitisation – all the challenges of the global community have been brought to the doorstep of the G20 in the hope that this group of powerful nations may find comity on the issues.

In 2020, the pandemic and a crisis of legitimacy at the World Health Organization added health to the G20's sky-high agenda.

The G20 community has striven to take all this in its stride. Under Saudi Arabia's leadership, the G20 has striven valiantly to contain damages wrought by the pandemic, spur economic recovery and

DOI: 10.4324/9781003152903-6

assist developing countries with a creative Debt Service Suspension Initiative (DSSI). Through virtual meetings throughout the year, the Saudi government generated a wealth of ideas, suggestions and recommendations through an elaborate process of consultations with the engagement groups of the G20, especially the T20 and the B20.

The Saudi Presidency has also worked hard to ensure a balance between handling the damaging impact of COVID on the one hand and the G20's regular agenda on the other hand. G20 ministers and officials have focused on seven clusters of themes relating to economic governance. These are finance, banking, trade and investment and infrastructure issues; the challenges of addressing inequality; improving the ecosystem for information technology and digitisation; climate change; terrorism financing; health-related issues and the war on COVID and the concerns of the Global South, particularly the G20's emerging partnership with Africa.

Italy, the G20 President in 2021, has been off to an energetic start – despite being one of the earliest and worst affected countries by the pandemic. Its B20 grouping is focused on reviving the SME sector, which contributes nearly 80% to its employment and 70% to its economy – themes central to the G20's core agenda. Less SDGs and more SMEs is a move towards the right track.

While the workings and influence of the G20 are less visible to the public, within governments of member-states, the G20's immense utility and relevance is clear and increasing. This information gap between the public and the state must be creatively and effectively addressed in order to raise the credibility of G20 as a whole.

India will have to consider this responsibility as readies for its G20 Presidency year in 2023. The country's leadership can start now to put in motion all its relevant limbs to ensure success – government, business, academia, innovators, people and media. For commensurate with its global vision and comprehensive national power, India is committed to making an appreciable contribution to the global good. With UN reform showing little signs of progress and with multilateral institutions created in the twentieth century continuing to underperform, India's interest and participation in the G20, an essentially twenty-first-century institution, must demonstrate that multilateralism can be both equitable and continue to deliver.

THE END

Bibliography

Al-Benyan, Yousef. "B20 Saudi Arabia, the Official Voice of the Private Sector to the G20, Welcomes the G20 Leaders' Commitment to Tackle the COVID-19 Pandemic." *B20 Saudi Arabia 2020*, 27 March 2020, accessed 18 January 2021, http://www.g20.utoronto.ca/b20/B20-welcomes-the-G20-Lea

B20. "B20 Tokyo Summit Joint Recommendations "Society 5.0 for SDGs", B20 Tokyo 2019." B20 Japan, 15 March 2019, accessed 19 January 2021, http://www.keidanren.or.jp/en/policy/2019/020_Recommendations.pdf

Başçi, Sıdıka and Durucan, Ayşegül. "A Review of Small and Medium Sized Enterprises (SMEs) in Turkey," *Yildiz Social Science Review*, 25 December 2017, accessed 20 January 2021, https://www.researchgate.net/publication/322437518_A_Review_of_Small_and_Medium_Sized_Enterprises_SMEs_in_Turkey#:~:text=SMEs%20play%20a%20very%20important, sustainable%20and%20balanced%20economic%20growth

Budget Speech by Nirmala Sitharman, Finance Minister of India, 1 February 2021, https://www.indiabudget.gov.in/budget2020-21/doc/Budget_Speech.pdf

Carin, Barry. "G20 Safeguards Vulnerabilities of Digital Economy, with Financial Sector Focus," *G20 Insights*, 10 December 2020, accessed 20 January 2021, https://www.g20-insights.org/policy_briefs/g20-safeguards-vulnerabilities-digital-economy-financial-sector-focus/

Chatzky, Andrew and McBride, James. "The Group of Twenty'." *Council on Foreign Relations*, 10 June 2019, accessed 18 January 2021, https://www.cfr.org/backgrounder/grouptwenty

Climate Action Network International. "G20 Working Group – Issue Briefs." *Climate Action Network International.* n.d., accessed 18 January 2021, http://www.climatenetwork.org/working-group-pages/g20

Deo, Neelam. "China's Influence over the UN." *Gateway House*, 05 July 2020, accessed 18 January 2021, https://www.gatewayhouse.in/chinas-influence-un/

European Commission. "2019 SBA Fact Sheet." *European Comission*, 2019, accessed 18 January 2021, https://ec.europa.eu/neighbourhood-enlargement/sites/near/files/sba-fs-2019_turkey.pdf

Fabricius, Peter. "G20 Compact with Africa Is a Long Game." Institute for Security Studies, 5 July 2019, accessed 18 January 2021, issafrica.org/iss-today/g20-compact-with-africa-is-a-long-game

FAQs about the G20, *G20 Germany 2017*, accessed 20 January 2021, https://www.g20germany.de/Webs/G20/EN/G20/FAQs/faq_node.html#:~:text=The%202017%20G20%20summit%20cost%20the%20German%20government%20%E2%82%AC%2072.2%20million

Floyd, Rob and Kapoor, Kapil. "G20 Compact with Africa." G20 Insights, 06 May 2020, accessed 18 January 2021, https://www.g20-insights.org/policy_briefs/g20-compact-with-africa/

G20. "G20 Compact with Africa." *G20 Compact with Africa.* n.d., accessed 19 January 2021, https://www.compactwithafrica.org/content/compactwithafrica/home.html

G20 Germany. "German Presidency at a Glance." *G20 Germany*, 2017, accessed 19 January 2021, https://www.g20germany.de/Webs/G20/EN/G20/Agenda/agenda_node.html#:~:text=Germany%20also%20wants%20to%20use, example%2C%20issues%20of%20global%20significance

G20. *G20 Italy Priorities*, 01 January, 2021, accessed 18 January 2021, https://www.g20.org/

G20 Saudi Arabia, G20 Leader's Declaration. Saudi Arabia: G20, 2020. https://www.ilo.org/global/about-the-ilo/how-the-ilo-works/multilateral-system/g20/WCMS_761761/lang--en/index.htm

G20 Turkey. "G20/OECD High-Level Principles on SME Financing." *G20 Antalya, Turkey.* accessed 18 January, 2021, https://ms.hmb.gov.tr/uploads/2018/11/Key-Messages.pdf

Gateway House. 'India and the G20' Based on Research by Gateway House for Ministry of Finance, November 2015.

Giri, Chaitanya. "India Must Back Developing World in Space20." *Gateway House*, 26 October 2020, accessed 18 January 2021, https://www.gatewayhouse.in/india-space20/

Global Infrastructure Hub, A G20 Initiative – https://www.gihub.org/

Goodman, Matthew. "Assessing the G20 Virtual Summit." *CSIS*, 27 March, 2020, accessed 18 January 2021, https://www.csis.org/analysis/assessing-g20-virtual-summit

GPFI. "G20 Action Plan on SME Financing Implementation Framework." *Global Partnership for Financial Inclusion*, 16 September 2016, accessed 20 January 2021, https://www.gpfi.org/publications/g20-action-plan-sme-financing-implementation-framework#:~:text=By%20endorsing%20the%20G20%20Action, through%20an%20enabling%20regulatory%20environment

Heger, Katrin and Downie, Richard, '. "Was the G20 Summit a "Win" for Africa?" Centre for Strategic and International Studies, 27 July 2017, accessed 18 January 2021, https://www.csis.org/analysis/was-g20-summit-win-africa

IMF. "Press Release: Inter-Agency Group on Economic and Financial Statistics Launches Enhanced G-20 Statistical Web Site, IMF Announces." *International Monetary Fund*, 22 December 2009, accessed 18 January

2021, https://www.imf.org/en/News/Articles/2015/09/14/01/49/pr09474#:~:-
text=The%20Inter%2DAgency%20Group%20on%20Economic%20
and%20Financial%20Statistics%20was, Nations%2C%20and%20the%20
World%20Bank

IMF-FSB. "Countdown to 2021 in Light of COVID-19." *International Monetary Fund.* October 2020, accessed 18 January 2021, https://www.imf.org/external/np/g20/pdf/2020/100720.pdf

Johns Hopkins University. "Coronavirus Global Map." *Johns Hopkins University Coronavirus Centre*, 18 January 2021, accessed 18 January 2021, https://coronavirus.jhu.edu/map.html

Leininger, Julia and others. "G20 and Africa – Ready for a Steady Partnership." *G20 Insights*, 19 October 2019, accessed 18 January 2021, https://www.g20-insights.org/policy_briefs/g20-africa-ready-steady-partnership/

Marco Felisati. "Speech Delivered on a Webinar 'G20's Future – Italy, Indonesia, India", *Gateway House – Konrad Adenauer Stiftung*, 14 January 2021, https://www.gatewayhouse.in/events/g20s-italy-indonesia-india/

Mathur, Akshay.

• "T20- Thinking for G20." *Gateway House – Indian Council on Global Relations*, 04 August 2016, accessed 18 January 2021, https://www.gatewayhouse.in/t20-thinking-g20/

• Modak, Purvaja and Bhandari, Amit. "A Decentralized, Consumer-driven Model for the Solar Eco-system," G20 Policy Brief, *G20 Insights*, 6 April 2017, accessed 19 January 2021, https://www.g20-insights.org/policy_briefs/decentralized-consumer-driven-model-solar-eco-system/

• Vaidyanathan, K N and Modak, Purvaja. "Mainstreaming Natural Capital Valuation," G20 Policy Brief, *G20 Insights*, 06 May 2019, accessed 18 January 2021, https://www.g20-insights.org/policy_briefs/mainstreaming-natural-capital-valuation/

• Mathur, Akshay, Vaidyanathan, K N and Modak, Purvaja. "A Global Framework for Tracing Beneficial Ownership," G20 Policy Brief, *G20 Insights*, 23 July 2019, accessed 19 January 2021, https://www.g20-insights.org/policy_briefs/a-global-framework-for-tracing-beneficial-ownership/

• Mathur, Akshay and Modak, Purvaja. "Measuring Cross-border Trade in Services by Trading Partner Country and Company," 5 April 2017, accessed 18 January 2021, https://www.g20-insights.org/policy_briefs/measuring-cross-border-trade-services-trading-partner-country-company/

• Mathur, Akshay. "Preparing India for the G20 Presidency in 2022," *Gateway House*, 31 January 2019, accessed 20 January 2021, https://www.gatewayhouse.in/india-g20-presidency/

Ministry of External Affairs, Government of India. "G20- Group of Twenty." *Ministry of External Affairs, Government of India*, August 2012, accessed 18 January 2021, http://www.mea.gov.in/Portal/ForeignRelation/g20-august-2012.pdf

Ministry of Statistics and Programme Implementation. "India, G20 and the World," *Ministry of Statistics and Programme Implementation, Government of India*, accessed 18 January 2021, http://mospi.nic.in/sites/default/files/Statistical_year_book_india_chapters/INDIA%2C%20G20%20AND%20THE%20WORLD%20-WRITEUP.PDF

Muhanna, Duja, "G20 Summit Costs, 2010–2018," *G20 Information Centre, University of Toronto*, 28 November 2018, accessed 20 January 2021, http://www.g20.utoronto.ca/factsheets/factsheet_costs-g20.html

OECD. *OECD-G20.* n.d., accessed 18 January 2021, https://www.oecd.org/g20/about/

OECD Policy Briefs. "Italian Regional SME Policy Responses." *OECD Trento Centre for Local Development of the OECD Centre for Entrepreneurship, SMEs, Regions and Cities (CFE)*, p. 4–5, 22 April 2020, accessed 20 January 2021, https://read.oecd-ilibrary.org/view/?ref=132_132736-237r9rskhm&title=Italian-regional-SME-policy-responses

Open letter to G20 Heads of State and Government', ICC and WHO." G20 Information Centre, University of Toronto, 23 March 2020, accessed 18 January 2021, http://www.g20.utoronto.ca/b20/2020-B20_WHO_and_ICC_joint_letter.pdf

Pai, T.V. Mohandas and Holla, Nisha. "India's Pioneering Tech-enabled Governance Model," 6 June 2020, accessed 20 January 2021, https://www.sundayguardianlive.com/business/indias-pioneering-tech-enabled-governance-model

Patrick, Stewart M. "'The Multilateral System Still Cannot Get Its Act Together on COVID-19'," *Council on Foreign Relation*, 26 March 2020, accessed 18 January 2021, https://www.cfr.org/blog/multilateral-system-still-cannot-get-its-act-together-covid-19

Press Information Bureau. "Government Unveils Vision for the Next Decade," *Ministry of Finance, Government of India*, 11 February 2019, accessed 20 January 2021, https://pib.gov.in/newsite/PrintRelease.aspx?relid=187925)

Press Release. "India's Trillion-Dollar Digital Opportunity," *Ministry of Electronics and Information Technology*, accessed 21 March 2020, https://www.meity.gov.in/writereaddata/files/india_trillion-dollar_digital_opportunity.pdf.

Rajan, Raghuram, Gateway House 25 October 2015, *T20 Mumbai Keynote by Dr. Rajan* https://www.gatewayhouse.in/t20-mumbai-keynote-by-dr-raghuram-rajan/

Sahbaz, Ussal. "Turkish Government Launches World SME Forum as Part of Its G20 Strategy," *International Chamber of Commerce*, 27 May 2015, accessed 20 January 2021, https://iccwbo.org/media-wall/news-speeches/turkish-government-launches-world-sme-forum-as-part-of-its-g20-strategy/

Speech by the King of the Kingdom of Saudi Arabia, "Saudi King's Message to G20," *G20 Saudi Arabia*, 1 December 2019, accessed 18 January 2021, https://g20.org/Documents/Presidency-King-Message.pdf?v=1

Trines, Stefan. "The State of Refugee Integration in Germany." *World Education News and Reviews*, 08 August 2019, accessed 18 January 2021, https://wenr.wes.org/2019/08/the-state-of-refugee-integration-in-germany-in-2019

UNECA. "'ECA: Three Things the G20 Must Do to Support Africa in the COVID-19 Pandemic," UNECA, 20 March 2020, accessed 18 January 2021, https://www.un.org/africarenewal/news/coronavirus/three-things-g20-must-do-support-africa-covid-19-pandemic

UNESCO. "In Historic Move, G20 Puts Culture on Its Agenda for the First Time." *UNESCO*, 06 November 2020, accessed 18 January 2021, https://en.unesco.org/news/historic-move-g20-putsculture-its-agenda-first-time

University of Toronto,

- Communiqué Virtual meeting of the G20 Finance Ministers and Central Bank Governors', Riyadh, Saudi Arabia. *G20Information Centre, University of Toronto*, 15 April 2020, accessed 18 January 2021.

- G20 Digital Economy Development and Cooperation Initiative, *G20 Information Centre*, 5 September 2016, http://www.g20.utoronto.ca/2016/160905-digital.html

- Extraordinary G20 Digital Economy Ministerial Meeting: COVID-19 Response Statement. *G20 Information Centre, University of Toronto*, 30 April 2020, accessed 18 January 2021, http://www.g20.utoronto.ca/2020/2020-g20-digital-0430.html

- "G20 Extraordinary Energy Ministers Meeting Statement." *G20 Information Centre, University of Toronto*, 10 April 2020, accessed 18 January 2021, http://www.g20.utoronto.ca/2020/2020-g20-energy-0410.html

- "G20 Information Centre – About Us." *University of Toronto, G20 Centre*. n.d., accessed 18 January 2021, http://www.g20.utoronto.ca/about.html

- "G20 Leaders Statement: The Pittsburgh Summit", *G20 Information Centre, University of Toronto*, http://www.g20.utoronto.ca/2009/2009communique0925.html

- "G20 Trade and Investment Ministerial Meeting: Ministerial Statement." *G20 Information Centre, University of Toronto*, 14 May 2020, accessed 18 January 2021, http://www.g20.utoronto.ca/2020/2020-g20-trade-0514.html

- 'Joint Statement on Employment, Skills & Women', B20, L20, W20. G20 Information Centre, University of Toronto, 5 April

2020, accessed 18 January 2021, http://www.g20.utoronto.ca/b20/B20-L20-W20-final-statement-2020.pdf

- "Press Release on the Extraordinary Virtual G20 Leaders' Summit." *G20 Information Centre, University of Toronto*, 26 March 2020, accessed 18 January 2021, http://www.g20.utoronto.ca/2020/2020-g20-modi-0326.html
- "Remarks at the G20 Extraordinary Leaders' Summit on COVID-19- Tedros Adhanom Ghebreyesus, Director General, World Health Organization." *G20 Information Centre, University of Toronto*, 26 March 2020, accessed 18 January 2021, http://www.g20.utoronto.ca/2020/2020-g20-tedros-0326.html
- 'Virtual Meeting of the G20 Finance Ministers and Central Bank Governors', Communiqué." G20 Information Centre, University of Toronto, 18 July 2020, accessed 18 January 2021, http://www.g20.utoronto.ca/2020/2020-g20-finance-0718.html
- "Working Together to Defeat the COVID-19 Outbreak – Statement by Xi Jinping." *G20 Information Centre, University of Toronto*. 26 March 2020, accessed 18 January 2021, http://www.g20.utoronto.ca/2020/2020-g20-xi-0326.html
- "'Paradise on Earth': China's Hangzhou Gets Propaganda Facelift for G20 Summit," *The Guardian*, 31 August 2016, accessed 20 January 2021, https://www.theguardian.com/world/2016/aug/31/china-hangzhou-propaganda-facelift-g20-summit

Urban20 Riyadh. *Circular Carbon Neutral Economy*, 2020, accessed 18 January 2021, https://www.urban20riyadh.org/taskforces/circular-carbon-neutral-economy

Webinar on 'G20's Future – Italy, Indonesia, India', *Gateway House – Konrad Adenauer Stiftung*, 14 January 2021, https://www.gatewayhouse.in/events/g20s-italy-indonesia-india/

World SME Forum http://www.worldsmeforum.org/about/

Yue, Wang. 'What We Know about China's G20 Host City Hangzhou," *Forbes*, 2 September 2016, accessed 20 January 2021, https://www.forbes.com/sites/ywang/2016/09/02/what-we-know-about-chinas-g20-summit-host-city-hangzhou/#228d86e175f7

Index

Note: **Bold** page numbers refer to tables; *italic* page numbers refer to figures and page numbers followed by "n" denote endnotes.

For Product Safety Concerns and Information please contact our EU
representative GPSR@taylorandfrancis.com
Taylor & Francis Verlag GmbH, Kaufingerstraße 24, 80331 München, Germany

For Product Safety Concerns and Information please contact our EU
representative GPSR@taylorandfrancis.com
Taylor & Francis Verlag GmbH, Kaufingerstraße 24, 80331 München, Germany

www.ingramcontent.com/pod-product-compliance
Lightning Source LLC
Chambersburg PA
CBHW061256220326
41599CB00028B/5673